ISBN-13: 9781772452112

Version 7.8 UPDATED March 2020

About Complete Test Preparation Inc.

The Complete Test Preparation Team has been publishing high quality study materials since 2005. Over two million students visit our websites every year, and thousands of students, teachers and parents all over the world (over 100 countries) have purchased our teaching materials, curriculum, study guides and practice tests.

Complete Test Preparation Inc. is committed to providing students with the best study materials and practice tests available on the market. Members of our team combine years of teaching experience, with experienced writers and editors, all with advanced degrees.

Feedback

Find us on Facebook

www.facebook.com/CompleteTestPreparation

CONTENTS

6 GETTING STARTED
    How this study guide is organized   7
    The PERT Study Plan   8
    Making a Study Schedule   8

14 READING COMPREHENSION
    Self-Assessment   15
    Answer Key   27
    Help with Reading Comprehension   30
    Main Idea and Supporting Details   33
    Drawing Inferences And Conclusions   37
    Meaning From Context   41
    Point Of View And Purpose   43

47 MATHEMATICS
    Self-Assessment   52
    Answer Key 57
    Solving One-Variable Linear Equations   65
    Solving Two-Variable Linear Equations   66
    Adding and Subtracting Polynomials 67
    Multiplying and Dividing Polynomials   68
    Simplifying Polynomials   69
    Factoring Polynomials   69
    Quadratic equations   70
    Basic Geometry   72
    Quadrilaterals 79

83 WRITING
    Self-Assessment   86
    Answer Key   95
    Common English Usage Mistakes   98
    Subject Verb Agreement   105
    Punctuation   111
    Hyphens   112
    Apostrophes   113
    Commas   114
    Quotation Marks   117
    English Grammar Multiple Choice   119

PERT
Study Guide

Postsecondary Education Readiness Test Study Guide and Practice Questions

COMPLETE
TEST PREPARATION INC.
WWW.TEST-PREPARATION.CA

Copyright © 2017 by Complete Test Preparation Inc. ALL RIGHTS RESERVED. No part of this book may be reproduced or transferred in any form or by any means, graphic, electronic, or mechanical, including photocopying, recording, web distribution, taping, or by any information storage retrieval system, without the written permission of the author.

Notice: Complete Test Preparation Inc. makes every reasonable effort to obtain from reliable sources accurate, complete, and timely information about the tests covered in this book. Nevertheless, changes can be made in the tests or the administration of the tests at any time and Complete Test Preparation Inc. makes no representation or warranty, either expressed or implied as to the accuracy, timeliness, or completeness of the information contained in this book. Complete Test Preparation Inc. makes no representations or warranties of any kind, express or implied, about the completeness, accuracy, reliability, suitability or availability with respect to the information contained in this document for any purpose. Any reliance you place on such information is therefore strictly at your own risk.

The author(s) shall not be liable for any loss incurred as a consequence of the use and application, directly or indirectly, of any information presented in this work. Sold with the understanding, the author(s) is not engaged in rendering professional services or advice. If advice or expert assistance is required, the services of a competent professional should be sought.

The company, product and service names used in this publication are for identification purposes only. All trademarks and registered trademarks are the property of their respective owners. Complete Test Preparation Inc. is not affiliated with any educational institution.

The PERT Exam is administered by the Florida Department of Education, who are not involved in the production of, and do not endorse this publication.

We strongly recommend that students check with exam providers for up-to-date information regarding test content.

137 HOW TO WRITE AN ESSAY
    Common Essay Mistakes - Example 1   147
    Common Essay Mistakes - Example 2   149
    Writing Concisely   152
    Avoiding Redundancy   154

161 PRACTICE TEST QUESTIONS SET 1
    Answer Key   201

220 PRACTICE TEST QUESTIONS SET 2
    Answer Key   257

281 ONLINE RESOURCES

282 CONCLUSION

160 REGISTER FOR FREE UPDATES

Getting Started

Congratulations! By deciding to take the Florida Post Secondary Readiness Test (PERT), you have taken the first step toward a great future! Of course, there is no point in taking this important examination unless you intend to do your best to earn the highest grade you possibly can. That means getting yourself organized and discovering the best approaches, methods and strategies to master the material. Yes, that will require real effort and dedication but if you are willing to focus your energy and devote the study time necessary, before you know it you will be on you will be opening that letter of acceptance to the school of your dreams!

We know that taking on a new endeavour can be a little scary, and it is easy to feel unsure of where to begin. That's where we come in. This study guide is designed to help you improve your test-taking skills, show you a few tricks of the trade and increase both your competency and confidence.

The PERT Exam

The PERT exam has three main sections, reading, mathematics, and writing. The reading section consists of reading comprehension, analysis of written passages and meaning in context. The mathematics section contains, arithmetic, algebra, geometry and polynomials and quadratic equations. The writing skills section contains questions on sentence structure and rewriting sentences. The writing section contains an essay question, as well as English grammar, spelling, punctuation and usage.

The PERT exam is computer based and adaptive. This means if you answer a questions correctly, the next question will be more difficulty until you reach your level of difficulty. If you answer incorrectly and you are not already at the lowest level of difficulty, the next question will be easier. Each question is multiple-choice, and the exact number of questions varies from student to student depending on how skilled the student is in a particular area.

While we seek to make our guide as comprehensive as possible, note that like all exams, the PERT Exam might be adjusted at some future point. New material might be added, or content that is no longer relevant or applicable might be removed. It is always a good idea to give the materials you receive when you register a careful review.

How This Study Guide is Organized

This study guide is divided into three sections. The first section, self-assessments, which will help you recognize your areas of strength and weaknesses. This will be a boon when it comes to managing your study time most efficiently; there is not much point of focusing on material you have already got firmly under control. Instead, taking the self-assessments will show you where that time could be much better spent. In this area you will begin with a few questions to evaluate quickly your understanding of material that is likely to appear on the PERT. If you do poorly in certain areas, simply work carefully through those sections in the tutorials and then try the self-assessment again.

The second section, Tutorials, offers information in each of the content areas, as well as strategies to help you master that material. The tutorials are not intended to be a complete course, but cover general principles. If you find that you do not understand the tutorials, it is recommended that you seek out additional instruction.

Third, we offer two sets of practice test questions, similar to those on the PERT Exam.

The PERT Study Plan

Now that you have made the decision to take the PERT, it is time to get started. Before you do another thing, you will need to figure out a plan of attack. The very best study tip is to start early! The longer the time period you devote to regular study practice, the more likely you will be to retain the material and access it quickly. If you thought that 1x20 is the same as 2x10, guess what? It really is not, when it comes to study time. Reviewing material for just an hour per day over the course of 20 days is far better than studying for two hours a day for only 10 days. The more often you revisit a particular piece of information, the better you will know it. Not only will your grasp and understanding be better, but your ability to reach into your brain and quickly and efficiently pull out the tidbit you need, will be greatly enhanced as well.

The great Chinese scholar and philosopher Confucius believed that true knowledge could be defined as knowing what you know and what you do not know. The first step in preparing for the PERT is to assess your strengths and weaknesses. You may already have an idea of what you know and what you do not know, but evaluating yourself using our Self- Assessment modules for each of the three areas, Math, Writing and Reading Comprehension, will clarify the details.

Making a Study Schedule

To make your study time the most productive, you will need to develop a study plan. The purpose of the plan is to organize all the bits of pieces of information in such a way that you will not feel overwhelmed. Rome was not built in a day, and learning everything you will need to know to pass the PERT is going to take time, too. Arranging the material you need to learn into manageable chunks is the best way to go. Each study session should make you feel as though you have reached your goal, and your goal is simply to learn what you planned to learn during that particular session. Try to organize the content in such a way that each study session builds on previous ones. That way, you will retain the information, be better able to access it, and review the previous bits and pieces at the same time.

Self-assessment

The Best Study Tip! The very best study tip is to start early! The longer you study regularly, the more you will retain and 'learn' the material. Studying for 1 hour per day for 20 days is far better than studying for 2 hours for 10 days.

What don't you know?

The first step is to assess your strengths and weaknesses. You may already have an idea of where your weaknesses are, or you can take our Self-assessment modules for each of the areas, Reading Comprehension, Arithmetic, Essay Writing, Algebra and College Level Math.

Exam Component	Rate 1 to 5
Reading Comprehension	
Making Inferences	
Main idea	
Arithmetic	
Decimals Percent and Fractions	
Problem solving (Word Problems)	
Basic Algebra	
Simple Geometry	
Problem Solving	

Essay and English	
Essay Writing	
Basic English Grammar and Usage	
Spelling	
Punctuation	
Capitalization	
Mathematics	
Linear Equations	
Quadratics	
Polynomials	
Coordinate Geometry	

Making a Study Schedule

The key to making a study plan is to divide the material you need to learn into manageable size and learn it, while at the same time reviewing the material that you already know.

Using the table above, any scores of three or below, you need to spend time learning, going over, and practicing this subject area. A score of four means you need to review the material, but you don't have to re-learn. A score of five and you are OK with just an occasional review before the exam.

A score of zero or one means you really do need to work on this and you should allocate the most time and give it the highest priority. Some students prefer a 5-day plan and others a 10-day plan. It also depends on how much time until the exam.

Here is an example of a 5-day plan based on an example from the table above:

Main Idea: 1   Study 1 hour everyday – review on last day
Linear Equations: 3   Study 1 hour for 2 days then ½ hour and then review
Algebra: 4   Review every second day
Grammar & Usage: 2 Study 1 hour on the first day – then ½ hour everyday

Getting Started

Reading Comprehension: 5 Review for ½ hour every other day
Geometry: 5 Review for ½ hour every other day

Using this example, geometry and reading comprehension are good and only need occasional review. Algebra is good and needs 'some' review. Linear Equations need a bit of work, grammar and usage needs a lot of work and Main Idea is very weak and need most of time.   Based on this, here is a sample study plan:

Day	Subject	Time
Monday		
Study	Main Idea	1 hour
Study	Grammar & Usage	1 hour
	½ hour break	
Study	Linear Equations	1 hour
Review	Algebra	½ hour
Tuesday		
Study	Main Idea	1 hour
Study	Grammar & Usage	½ hour
	½ hour break	
Study	Linear Equations	½ hour
Review	Algebra	½ hour
Review	Geometry	½ hour
Wednesday		
Study	Main Idea	1 hour
Study	Grammar & Usage	½ hour
	½ hour break	
Study	Linear Equations	½ hour
Review	Geometry	½ hour
Thursday		
Study	Main Idea	½ hour
Study	Grammar & Usage	½ hour
Review	Linear Equations	½ hour
	½ hour break	
Review	Geometry	½ hour
Review	Algebra	½ hour

Friday		
Review	Main Idea	½ hour
Review	Grammar & Usage	½ hour
Review	Linear Equations	½ hour
	½ hour break	
Review	Algebra	½ hour
Review	Grammar & Usage	½ hour

Using this example, adapt the study plan to your own schedule. This schedule assumes 2 ½ - 3 hours available to study everyday for a 5 day period.

First, write out what you need to study and how much. Next figure out how many days before the test. Note, do NOT study on the last day before the test. On the last day before the test, you won't learn anything and will probably only confuse yourself.

Make a table with the days before the test and the number of hours you have available to study each day. We suggest working with 1 hour and ½ hour time slots.

Start filling in the blanks, with the subjects you need to study the most, getting the most time, and the most regular time slots (i.e. everyday) and the subjects that you know getting the least time (e.g. ½ hour every other day, or every 3rd day).

Tips for making a schedule

Once you make a schedule, stick with it! Make your study sessions reasonable. If you make a study schedule and don't stick with it, you set yourself up for failure. Instead, schedule study sessions that are a bit shorter and set yourself up for success! Make sure your study sessions are do-able. Studying is hard work, but after you pass, you can party and take a break!

Schedule breaks. Breaks are just as important as study time. Work out a rotation of studying and breaks that works for you.

Build up study time. If you find it hard to sit still and study for 1 hour straight through, build up to it. Start with 20 minutes, and then take a break. Once you get used to 20-minute study sessions, increase the time to 30 minutes. Gradually work you way up to 1 hour.

How to Make a Study Plan and Schedule
https://www.test-preparation.ca/make-study-plan/

40 minutes to 1 hour are optimal. Studying for longer than this is tiring and not productive. Studying for shorter isn't long enough to be productive.

Studying Math. Studying Math is different from studying other subjects because you use a different part of your brain. The best way to study math is to practice everyday. This will train your mind to think in a mathematical way. If you miss a day or days, the mathematical mind-set is gone and you have to start all over again to build it up.

More on how to study math
https://www.test-preparation.ca/how-to-study-for-a-math-test-the-complete-guide/

How to Study
For more information, see our How to Study Guide at
https://www.test-preparation.ca/learning-study/

Reading Comprehension

This section contains a self-assessment and reading tutorial. The tutorials are designed to familiarize general principles and the self-assessment contains general questions similar to the reading questions likely to be on the PERT, but are not intended to be identical to the exam questions. The tutorials are not designed to be a complete reading course, and it is assumed that students have some familiarity with reading comprehension questions. If you do not understand parts of the tutorial, or find the tutorial difficult, it is recommended that you seek out additional instruction.

Tour of the PERT Reading Comprehension Content

Below is a more detailed list of the types of reading comprehension questions that generally appear on the PERT. Make sure you understand all of these points at a very minimum.

- Draw logical conclusions
- Identify the main idea
- Identify secondary ideas
- Identify the author's intent
- Summarizing
- Identify tone
- Distinguish between fact and opinion

The questions below are not the same as you will find on the PERT - that would be too easy! And nobody knows what the questions will be and they change all the time. Mostly the changes consist of substituting new questions for old, but the changes can be new question formats or styles, changes to the number of questions in each section, changes to the time limits for each section and combining sections. Below are general reading questions that cover the same areas as the PERT. While the format and exact wording of the questions may differ slightly, and change from year to year, if you can answer the questions below, you will have no problem with the reading section of the PERT.

Reading Comprehension Self-Assessment

The purpose of the self-assessment is:

- Identify your strengths and weaknesses.
- Develop your personalized study plan (above)
- Get accustomed to the PERT format
- Extra practice – the self-assessments are almost a full 3rd practice test!
- Provide a baseline score for preparing your study schedule.

Since this is a Self-assessment, and depending on how confident you are with Reading Comprehension, timing is optional. A general rule is one minute per question, so allow 25 minutes to complete this self-assessment. Once complete, use the table below to assess your understanding of the content, and prepare your study schedule described in chapter 1.

80% - 100%	Excellent – you have mastered the content
60 – 79%	Good. You have a working knowledge. Even though you can just pass this section, you may want to review the tutorials and do some extra practice to see if you can improve your mark.
40% - 59%	Below Average. You do not understand the reading comprehension problems. Review the tutorials, and retake this quiz again in a few days, before proceeding to the practice test questions.
Less than 40%	Poor. You have a very limited understanding of the reading comprehension problems. Please review the tutorials, and retake this quiz again in a few days, before proceeding to the practice test questions.

Reading Self-Assessment

	A	B	C	D
1	○	○	○	○
2	○	○	○	○
3	○	○	○	○
4	○	○	○	○
5	○	○	○	○
6	○	○	○	○
7	○	○	○	○
8	○	○	○	○
9	○	○	○	○
10	○	○	○	○
11	○	○	○	○
12	○	○	○	○
13	○	○	○	○
14	○	○	○	○
15	○	○	○	○
16	○	○	○	○

Directions: The following questions are based on several reading passages. A series of questions follow each passage. Read each passage carefully, and then answer the questions based on it. You may reread the passage as often as you wish. When you have finished answering the questions based on one passage, go right onto the next passage. Choose the best answer based on the information given and implied.

Questions 1 – 4 refer to the following passage.

Passage 1 - Who Was Anne Frank?

You may have heard mention of the word Holocaust in your History or English classes. The Holocaust took place from 1939-1945. It was an attempt by the Nazi party to purify the human race, by eliminating Jews, Gypsies, Catholics, homosexuals and others they deemed inferior to their "perfect" Aryan race. The Nazis used Concentration Camps, which were sometimes used as Death Camps, to exterminate the people they held in the camps. The saddest fact about the Holocaust was the over one million children under the age of sixteen died in a Nazi concentration camp. Just a few weeks before World War II was over, Anne Frank was one of those children to die.

Before the Nazi party began its persecution of the Jews, Anne Frank had a happy live. She was born in June of 1929. In June of 1942, for her 13th birthday, she was given a simple present which would go onto impact the lives of millions of people around the world. That gift was a small red diary that she called Kitty. This diary was to become Anne's most treasured possession when she and her family hid from the Nazi's in a secret annex above her father's office building in Amsterdam.

For 25 months, Anne, her sister Margot, her parents, another family, and an elderly Jewish dentist hid from the Nazis in this tiny annex. They were never permitted to go outside, and their food and supplies were brought to them by Miep Gies and her husband, who did not believe in the Nazi persecution of the Jews. It was a very difficult life for young Anne and she used Kitty as an outlet to describe her life in hiding.

After 2 years, Anne and her family were betrayed and arrested by the Nazis. To this day, nobody is exactly sure who betrayed the Frank family and the other annex residents. Anne, her mother, and her sister were separated from Otto Frank, Anne's father. Then, Anne and Margot were separated from their mother. In March of 1945, Margot Frank died of starvation in a Concentration Camp. A few days later, at the age of 15, Anne Frank died of typhus. Of all the people who hid in the Annex, only Otto Frank survived the Holocaust.

Otto Frank returned to the Annex after World War II. It was there that he found Kitty, filled with Anne's thoughts and feelings about being a persecuted Jewish girl. Otto Frank had Anne's diary published in 1947 and it has remained continuously in print ever since. Today, the diary has been published in over 55 languages and more than 24 million copies have been sold around the world. The Diary of Anne Frank tells the story of a brave young woman who tried to see the good in all people.

1. From the context clues in the passage, what does annex mean?

    a. Attic

    b. Bedroom

    c. Basement

    d. Kitchen

2. Why do you think Anne's diary has been published in 55 languages?

a. So everyone could understand it.

b. So people around the world could learn more about the horrors of the Holocaust.

c. Because Anne was Jewish but hid in Amsterdam and died in Germany.

d. Because Otto Frank spoke many languages.

3. From the description of Anne and Margot's deaths in the passage, what can we assume typhus is?

a. The same as starving to death.

b. An infection the Germans gave to Anne.

c. A disease Anne caught in the concentration camp.

d. Poison gas used by the Germans to kill Anne.

4. In the third paragraph, what does outlet mean?

a. A place to plug things into the wall

b. A store where Miep bought cheap supplies for the Frank family

c. A hiding space similar to an Annex

d. A place where Anne could express her private thoughts.

Questions 5 – 8 refer to the following passage.

Passage 2 - Was Dr. Seuss A Real Doctor?

A favorite author for over 100 years, Theodor Seuss Geisel was born on March 2, 1902. Today, we celebrate the birthday of the famous "Dr. Seuss" by hosting Read Across America events throughout the March. School children around the country celebrate the "Doctor's" birthday by making hats, giving presentations and holding read aloud circles featuring some of Dr. Seuss' most famous books.

But who was Dr. Seuss? Did he go to medical school? Where was his office? You may be surprised to know that Theodor Seuss Geisel was not a medical doctor at all. He took on the nickname Dr. Seuss when he became a noted children's book author. He earned the nickname because people said his books were "as good as medicine." All these years later, his nickname has lasted and he is known as Dr. Seuss all across the world.

Think back to when you were a young child. Did you ever want to try "green eggs and ham?" Did you try to "Hop on Pop?" Do you remember learning about the environment from a creature called The Lorax? Of course, you must recall one of Seuss' most famous characters; that green Grinch who stole Christmas. These stories were all written by Dr. Seuss and featured his signature rhyming words and letters. They also featured made up words to enhance his rhyme scheme and even though many of his characters were made up, they sure seem real to us today.

And what of his "signature" book, The Cat in the Hat? You must remember that cat and Thing One and Thing Two from your childhood. Did you know that in the early 1950's there was a growing concern in America that children were not becoming avid readers? This was, book publishers thought, because children found books dull and uninteresting. An intelligent publisher sent Dr. Seuss a book of words that he thought all children should learn as young readers. Dr. Seuss wrote his famous story The Cat in the Hat, using those words. We can see, over the decades, just how much influence his writing has had on very young children. That is why we celebrate this doctor's birthday each March.

5. What does the word "avid" mean in the last paragraph?

      a. Good

      b. Interested

      c. Slow

      d. Fast

6. What can we infer from the statement "His books were like medicine?"

   a. His books made people feel better

   b. His books were in doctor's office waiting rooms

   c. His books took away fevers

   d. His books left a funny taste in readers' mouths.

7. Why is the publisher in the last paragraph called "intelligent?"

   a. The publisher knew how to read.

   b. The publisher knew that kids did not like to read.

   c. The publisher knew Dr. Seuss would be able to create a book that sold well.

   d. The publisher knew that Dr. Seuss would be able to write a book that would get young children interested in reading.

8. The theme of this passage is

   a. Dr. Seuss was not a doctor.

   b. Dr. Seuss influenced the lives of generations of young children.

   c. Dr. Seuss wrote rhyming books.

   d. Dr. Suess' birthday is a good day to read a book.

Questions 9 - 12 refer to the following passage.

Keeping Tropical Fish

Keeping tropical fish at home or in your office used to be very popular. Today, interest has declined, but it remains as rewarding and relaxing a hobby as ever. Ask any tropical fish hobbyist, and you will hear how soothing and relaxing watching colorful fish live their lives in the aquarium. If you are considering keeping tropical fish as pets, here is a list of the basic equipment you will need.

A filter is essential for keeping your aquarium clean and your fish alive and healthy. There are different types and sizes of filters and the right size for you depends on the size of the aquarium and the level of stocking. Generally, you need a filter with a 3 to 5 times turn over rate per hour. This means that the water in the tank should go through the filter about 3 to 5 times per hour.

Most tropical fish do well in water temperatures ranging between 24° C and 26° C, though each has its own ideal water temperature. A heater with a thermostat is necessary to regulate the water temperature. Some heaters are submersible and others are not, so check carefully before you buy.

Lights are also necessary, and come in a large variety of types, strengths and sizes. A light source is necessary for plants in the tank to photosynthesize and give the tank a more attractive appearance. Even if you plan to use plastic plants, the fish still require light, although here you can use a lower strength light source.

A hood is necessary to keep dust, dirt and unwanted materials out of the tank. Sometimes the hood can also help prevent evaporation. Another requirement is aquarium gravel. This will improve the aesthetics of the aquarium and is necessary if you plan to have real plants.

9. What is the general tone of this article?

    a. Formal

    b. Informal

    c. Technical

    d. Opinion

10. Which of the following cannot be inferred?

   a. Gravel is good for aquarium plants.

   b. Fewer people have aquariums in their office than at home.

   c. The larger the tank, the larger the filter required.

   d. None of the above.

11. What evidence does the author provide to support their claim that aquarium lights are necessary?

   a. Plants require light.

   b. Fish and plants require light.

   c. The author does not provide evidence for this statement.

   d. Aquarium lights make the aquarium more attractive.

12. Which of the following is an opinion?

   a. Filter with a 3 to 5 times turn over rate per hour are required.

   b. Aquarium gravel improves the aesthetics of the aquarium.

   c. An aquarium hood keeps dust, dirt and unwanted materials out of the tank.

   d. Each type of tropical fish has its own ideal water temperature.

Questions 13 - 16 refer to the following passage.

The Civil War

The Civil War began on April 12, 1861. The first shots of the Civil War were fired in Fort Sumter, South Carolina. Note that even though more American lives were lost in the Civil

Reading Comprehension

War than in any other war, not one person died on that first day. The war began because eleven Southern states seceded from the Union and tried to start their own government, The Confederate States of America.

Why did the states secede? The issue of slavery was a primary cause of the Civil War. The eleven southern states relied heavily on their slaves to foster their farming and plantation lifestyles. The northern states, many of whom had already abolished slavery, did not feel that the southern states should have slaves. The north wanted to free all the slaves and President Lincoln's goal was to both end slavery and preserve the Union. He had Congress declare war on the Confederacy on April 14, 1862. For four long, blood soaked years, the North and South fought.

From 1861 to mid 1863, it seemed as if the South would win this war. However, on July 1, 1863, an epic three day battle was waged on a field in Gettysburg, Pennsylvania. Gettysburg is remembered for being the bloodiest battle in American history. At the end of the three days, the North turned the tide of the war in their favor. The North then went on to dominate the South for the remainder of the war. Another famous event is General Sherman's "March to The Sea," where he famously led the Union Army through Georgia and the Carolinas, burning and destroying everything in their path.
In 1865, the Union army invaded and captured the Confederate capital of Richmond Virginia. Robert E. Lee, leader of the Confederacy surrendered to General Ulysses S. Grant, leader of the Union forces, on April 9, 1865. The Civil War was over and the Union was preserved.

13. What does secede mean?

    a. To break away from

    b. To accomplish

    c. To join

    d. To lose

14. Which of the following statements summarizes a FACT from the passage?

    a. Congress declared war and then the Battle of Fort Sumter began.

    b. Congress declared war after shots were fired at Fort Sumter.

    c. President Lincoln was pro slavery

    d. President Lincoln was at Fort Sumter with Congress

15. Which event finally led the Confederacy to surrender?

    a. The battle of Gettysburg

    b. The battle of Bull Run

    c. The invasion of the confederate capital of Richmond

    d. Sherman's March to the Sea

16. What does the word abolish as used in this passage mean?

    a. To ban

    b. To polish

    c. To support

    d. To destroy

Answer Key

1. A
We know that an annex is like an attic because the text states the annex was above Otto Frank's building.

Choice B is incorrect because an office building doesn't have bedrooms. Choice C is incorrect because a basement would be below the office building. Choice D is incorrect because there would not be a kitchen in an office building.

2. B
The diary has been published in 55 languages so people all over the world can learn about Anne. That is why the passage says it has been continuously in print.

Choice A is incorrect because it is too vague. Choice C is incorrect because it was published after Anne died and she did not write in all three languages. Choice D is incorrect because the passage does not give us any information about what languages Otto Frank spoke.

3. C
Use the process of elimination to figure this out.

Choice A cannot be the correct answer because otherwise, the passage would have simply said that Anne and Margot both died of starvation. Choices B and D cannot be correct because, if the Germans had done something specifically to murder Anne, the passage would have stated that directly. By the process of elimination, choice C has to be the correct answer.

4. D
We can figure this out using context clues. The paragraph is talking about Anne's diary and so, outlet in this instance is a place where Anne can pour her feelings.

Choice A is incorrect answer. That is the literal meaning of the word outlet and the passage is using the figurative meaning. Choice B is incorrect because that is the secondary literal meaning of the word outlet, as in an outlet mall. Again, we are looking for figurative meaning. Choice C is incorrect because

there are no clues in the text to support that answer.
5. B
When someone is avid about something that means they are highly interested in the subject. The context clues are dull and boring, because they define the opposite of avid.

6. A
The author is using a simile to compare the books to medicine. Medicine is what you take when you want to feel better. They are suggesting that if you want to feel good, they should read Dr. Seuss' books.

Choice B is incorrect because there is no mention of a doctor's office. Choice C is incorrect because it is using the literal meaning of medicine and the author is using medicine in a figurative way. Choice D is incorrect because it makes no sense. We know not to eat books.

7. D
The publisher is described as intelligent because he knew to get in touch with a famous author to develop a book that children would be interested in reading.

Choice A is incorrect because we can assume that all book publishers must know how to read. Choice B is incorrect because it says in the article that more than one publisher was concerned whether children liked to read. Choice D is incorrect because there is no mention in the article about how well The Cat in the Hat sold when it was first published.

8. B
The passage describes in detail how Dr. Seuss had a great effect on the lives of children through his writing. It names several of his books, tells how he helped children become avid readers and explains his style of writing.

Choice A is incorrect because that is just one single fact about the passage. Choice C is incorrect because that is just one single fact about the passage. Choice D is incorrect because that is just one single fact about the passage. Again, choice B is correct because it encompasses ALL the facts in the passage, not just one single fact.

Reading Comprehension

9. B
The general tone is informal.

10. B
The statement, "Fewer people have aquariums in their office than at home," cannot be inferred from this article.

11. B
Light is necessary for the fish and plants.

12. B
The following statement is an opinion, " Aquarium gravel improves the aesthetics of the aquarium."

13. A
Secede means to break away from because the 11 states wanted to leave the United States and form their own country.

Choice B is incorrect because the states were not accomplishing anything. Choice C is incorrect because the states were trying to leave the USA not join it. Choice D is incorrect because the states seceded before they lost the war.

14. B
Look at the dates in the passage. The shots were fired on April 12 and Congress declared war on April 14.

Choice C is incorrect because the passage states that Lincoln was against slavery. Choice D is incorrect because it never mentions who was or was not at Fort Sumter.

15. C
The passage states that Lee surrendered to Grant after the capture of the capital of the Confederacy, which is Richmond.

Choice A is incorrect because the war continued for 2 years after Gettysburg. Choice B is incorrect because that battle is not mentioned in the passage. Choice D is incorrect because the capture of the capital occurred after the march to the sea.

16. A
When the passage said that the North had *abolished* slavery, it implies that slaves were no longer allowed in the North. In essence slavery was banned.

Choice B makes no sense relative to the context of the passage. Choice C is incorrect because we know the North was fighting slavery, not for it. Choice D is incorrect because slavery is not a tangible thing that can be destroyed. It is a practice that had to be outlawed or banned.

HELP WITH READING COMPREHENSION

At first sight, reading comprehension tests look challenging especially if you are given long essays to answer only two to three questions. While reading, you might notice your attention wandering, or you may feel sleepy. Do not be discouraged because there are various tactics and long range strategies that make comprehending even long, boring essays easier.

Your friends before your foes. It is always best to tackle essays or passages with familiar subjects rather than those with unfamiliar ones. This approach applies the same logic as tackling easy questions before hard ones. Skip passages that do not interest you and leave them for later when there is more time.

Don't use 'special' reading techniques. This is not the time for speed-reading or anything like that – just plain ordinary reading – not too slow and not too fast.

Read through the entire passage and the questions before you do anything. Many students try reading the questions first and then looking for answers in the passage thinking this approach is more efficient. What these students do not realize is that it is often hard to navigate in unfamiliar roads. If you do not familiarize yourself with the passage first, looking for answers become not only time-consuming but also dangerous because you might miss the

Reading Comprehension

context of the answer you are looking for. If you read the questions first you will only confuse yourself and lose valuable time.

Familiarize yourself with reading comprehension questions. If you are familiar with the common types of reading questions, you are able to take note of important parts of the passage, saving time. There are six major kinds of reading questions.

- **Main Idea** - Questions that ask for the central thought or significance of the passage.

- **Specific Details** - Questions that asks for explicitly stated ideas.

- **Drawing Inferences** - Questions that ask for a statement's intended meaning.

- **Tone or Attitude** - Questions that test your ability to sense the emotional state of the author.

- **Context Meaning** – Questions that ask for the meaning of a word depending on the context.

- **Technique** – Questions that ask for the method of organization or the writing style of the author.

Read. Read. Read. The best preparation for reading comprehension tests is always to read, read and read. If you are not used to reading lengthy passages, you will probably lose concentration. Increase your attention span by making a habit out of reading.

Reading Comprehension tests become less daunting when you have trained yourself to read and understand fast. Always remember that it is easier to understand passages you are interested in. Do not read through passages hastily. Make mental notes of ideas that you think might be asked.

Reading Strategy

When facing the reading comprehension section of a standardized test, you need a strategy to be successful. You want to keep several steps in mind:

- **First, make a note of the time and the number of sections**. Time your work accordingly. Typically, four to five minutes per section is sufficient. Second, read the directions for each selection thoroughly before beginning (and listen well to any additional verbal instructions, as they will often clarify obscure or confusing written guidelines). You must know exactly how to do what you're about to do!

- **Now you're ready to begin reading the selection**. Read the passage carefully, noting significant characters or events on a scratch sheet of paper or underlining on the test sheet. Many students find making a basic list in the margins helpful. Quickly jot down or underline one-word summaries of characters, notable happenings, numbers, or key ideas. This will help you better retain information and focus wandering thoughts. Remember, however, that your main goal in doing this is to find the information that answers the questions. Even if you find the passage interesting, remember your goal and work fast but stay on track.

- **Now read the question and all of the choices.** Now you have read the passage, have a general idea of the main ideas, and have marked the important points. Read the question and all of the choices. Never choose an answer without reading them all! Questions are often designed to confuse – stay focussed and clear. Usually the answer choices will focus on one or two facts or inferences from the passage. Keep these clear in your mind.

- **Search for the answer**. With a very general idea of what the different choices are, go back to the passage and scan for the relevant information. Watch for big words, unusual or unique words. These make your job easier as you can scan the text for the particular word.

• **Mark the Answer**. Now you have the key information the question is looking for. Go back to the question, quickly scan the choices and mark the correct one.

Understand and practice the different types of standardized reading comprehension tests. See the list above for the different types. Typically, there will be several questions dealing with facts from the selection, a couple more inference questions dealing with logical consequences of those facts, and periodically an application-oriented question surfaces to force you to make connections with what you already know. Some students prefer to answer the questions as listed, and feel classifying the question and then ordering is wasting precious time. Other students prefer to answer the different types of questions in order of how easy or difficult they are. The choice is yours and do whatever works for you. If you want to try answering in order of difficulty, here is a recommended order, answer fact questions first; they're easily found within the passage. Tackle inference problems next, after re-reading the question(s) as many times as you need to. Application or 'best guess' questions usually take the longest, so save them for last.

Use the practice tests to try out both ways of answering and see what works for you.

For more help with reading comprehension, see Multiple Choice Secrets book at www.multiple choice.ca.

Main Idea and Supporting Details

Identifying the main idea, topic and supporting details in a passage can feel like an overwhelming task. The passages used for standardized tests can be boring and seem difficult - Test writers don't use interesting passages or ones that talk about things most people are familiar with. Despite these obstacles, all passages and paragraphs will have the information you need to answer the questions.

The topic of a passage or paragraph is its subject. It's the general idea and can be summed up in a word or short phrase. On some standardized tests, there is a short description of the passage if it's taken from a longer work. Make sure you read the description as it might state the topic of the passage. If not, read the passage and ask yourself, "Who or what is this about?" For example:

> Over the years, school uniforms have been hotly debated. Arguments are made that students have the right to show individuality and express themselves by choosing their own clothes. However, this brings up social and academic issues. Some kids cannot afford to wear the clothes they like and might be bullied by the "better dressed" students. With attention drawn to clothes and the individual, students will lose focus on class work and the reason they are in school. School uniforms should be mandatory.

Ask: What is this paragraph about?

Topic: school uniforms

Once you have the topic, it's easier to find the main idea. The main idea is a specific statement telling what the writer wants you to know about the topic. Writers usually state the main idea as a thesis statement. If you're looking for the main idea of a single paragraph, the main idea is called the topic sentence and will probably be the first or last sentence. If you're looking for the main idea of an entire passage, look for the thesis statement in either the first or last paragraph. The main idea is usually restated in the conclusion. To find the main idea of a passage or paragraph, follow these steps:

> 1. Find the topic.
>
> 2. Ask yourself, "What point is the author trying to make about the topic?"

Reading Comprehension

3. Create your own sentence summarizing the author's point.

4. Look in the text for the sentence closest in meaning to yours.

Look at the example paragraph again. It's already established that the topic of the paragraph is school uniforms. What is the main idea/topic sentence?

Ask: "What point is the author trying to make about school uniforms?"

Summary: Students should wear school uniforms.

Topic sentence: School uniforms should be mandatory.

Main Idea: School uniforms should be mandatory.

Each paragraph offers supporting details to explain the main idea. The details could be facts or reasons, but they will always answer a question about the main idea. What? Where? Why? When? How? How much/many? Look at the example paragraph again. You'll notice that more than one sentence answers a question about the main idea. These are the supporting details.

Main Idea: School uniforms should be mandatory.

Ask: Why? Some kids cannot afford to wear clothes they like and could be bullied by the "better dressed" kids. Supporting Detail

With attention drawn to clothes and the individual, Students will lose focus on class work and the reason they are in school. Supporting Detail

What if the author doesn't state the main idea in a topic sentence? The passage will have an implied main idea. It's not as difficult to find as it might seem. Paragraphs are always organized around ideas. To find an implied main idea, you need to know the topic and then find the relationship between the supporting details. Ask yourself, "What is the point the author is making about the relationship between the details?"

Cocoa is what makes chocolate good for you. Chocolate comes in many varieties. These delectable flavors include milk chocolate, dark chocolate, semi-sweet, and white chocolate.

Ask: What is this paragraph about?
Topic: Chocolate
Ask: What? Where? Why? When? How? How much/many?

Supporting details: Chocolate is good for you because it is made of cocoa, Chocolate is delicious, Chocolate comes in different delicious flavors

Ask: What is the relationship between the details and what is the author's point?

Main Idea: Chocolate is good because it is healthy and it tastes good.

Testing Tips for Main Idea Questions

1. Skim the questions – not the answer choices - before reading the passage.

2. Questions about main idea might use the words "theme," "generalization," or "purpose."

3. Save questions about the main idea for last. On standardized tests like the SAT, the answers to the rest of the questions can be found in order in the passage.

3. Underline topic sentences in the passage. Most tests allow you to write in your test booklet.

4. Answer the question in your own words before looking at the answer choices. Then match your answer with an answer choice.

5. Cross out incorrect answer choices immediately to prevent confusion.

6. If two of the answer choices mean the same thing but use different words, they are BOTH incorrect.

Reading Comprehension

7. If a question asks about the whole passage, cross out the answer choices that apply only to part of it.

8. If only part of the information is correct, that answer choice is incorrect.

9. An answer choice that is too broad is incorrect. All information needs to be backed up by the passage.

10. Answer choices with extreme wording are usually incorrect.

DRAWING INFERENCES AND CONCLUSIONS

Drawing inferences and making conclusions happens all the time. In fact, you probably do it every time you read—sometimes without even realizing it! For example, remember the first time you saw the movie "The Lion King." When you meet Scar for the first time, he is trapping a helpless mouse with his sharp claws preparing to eat it. When you see this action you guess that Scar is going to be the bad character in the movie. Nothing appeared to tell you this. No caption came across the bottom of the screen that said "Bad Guy." No red arrow pointed to Scar and said "Evil Lion." No, you made an inference about his character based on the context clue you were given. You do the same thing when you read!

When you draw an inference or make a conclusion you are doing the same thing—you are making an educated guess based on the hints the author gives you. We call these hints "context clues." Scar trapping the innocent mouse is the context clue about Scar's character.

Usually you are making inferences and drawing conclusions the entire time you are reading. Whether you realize it or not, you are constantly making educated guesses based on context clues. Think about a time you were reading a book and something happened that you were expecting to happen. You're not psychic! Actually, you were picking up on the context clues and making inferences about what was going to happen next!

Let's try an easy example. Read the following sentences and answer the questions at the end of the passage.

> Shelly really likes to help people. She loves her job because she gets to help people every single day. However, Shelly has to work long hours and she can get called in the middle of the night for emergencies. She wears a white lab coat at work and usually she carries a stethoscope.

What is Shelly's job?

a. Musician
b. Lawyer
c. Doctor
d. Teacher

This probably seemed easy. Drawing inferences isn't always this simple, but it is the same basic principle. How did you know Shelly was a doctor? She helps people, she works long hours, she wears a white lab coat, and she gets called in for emergencies at night. Context Clues! Nowhere in the paragraph did it say Shelly was a doctor, but you were able to draw that conclusion based on the information provided in the paragraph.

There is a catch, though. Remember that when you draw inferences based on reading, you should only use the information given to you by the author. Sometimes it is easy for us to make conclusions based on knowledge that is already in our mind—but that can lead you to drawing an incorrect inference. For example, let's pretend there is a bully at your school named Brent. Now let's say you read a story and the main character's name is Brent. You could NOT infer that the character in the story is a bully just because his name is Brent. You should only use the information given to you by the author to avoid drawing the wrong conclusion.

Reading Comprehension

Let's try another example.

> Social media is an extremely popular new form of connecting and communicating over the internet. Since Facebook's original launch in 2004, millions of people have joined in the social media craze. In fact, it is estimated that almost 75% of all internet users aged 18 and older use some form of social media. Facebook started at Harvard University as a way to get students connected. However, it quickly grew into a worldwide phenomenon and today, the founder of Facebook, Mark Zuckerberg has an estimated net worth of 28.5 billion dollars.
>
> Facebook is not the only social media platform, though. Other sites such as Twitter, Instagram, and Snapchat have since been invented and are quickly becoming just as popular! Many social media users actually use more than one type of social media. Furthermore, most social media sites have created mobile apps that allow people to connect via social media virtually anywhere in the world!

What is the most likely reason that other social media sites like Twitter and Instagram were created?

> a. Professors at Harvard University made it a class project.
>
> b. Facebook was extremely popular and other people thought they could also be successful by designing social media sites.
>
> c. Facebook was not connecting enough people.
>
> d. Mark Zuckerberg paid people to invent new social media sites because he wanted lots of competition.

Here, the correct answer is B. Facebook was extremely popular and other people thought they could also be successful by designing social media sites. How do we know this? What are the context clues? Take a look at the first paragraph. What do we know based on this paragraph?

Well, one sentence refers to Facebook's original launch. This suggests that Facebook was one of the first social media sites. In addition, we know that the founder of Facebook has been extremely successful and is worth billions of dollars. From this we can infer that other people wanted to imitate Facebook's idea and become just as successful as Mark Zuckerberg.

Let's go through the other answers. If you chose A, it might be because Facebook started at Harvard University, so you drew the conclusion that all other social media sites were also started at Harvard University. However, there is no mention of class projects, professors, or students designing social media. So there doesn't seem to be enough support for choice A.

If you chose C, you might have been drawing your own conclusions based on outside information. Maybe none of your friends are on Facebook, so you made an inference that Facebook didn't connect enough people, so more sites were invented. Or maybe you think the people who connect on Facebook are too old, so you don't think Facebook connects enough people your age. This might be true, but remember inferences should be drawn from the information the author gives you!

If you chose D, you might be using the information that Mark Zuckerberg is worth over 28 billion dollars. It would be easy for him to pay others to design new sites, but remember, you need to use context clues! He is very wealthy, but that statement was giving you information about how successful Facebook was—not suggesting that he paid others to design more sites!

So remember, drawing inferences and conclusions is simply about using the information you are given to make an educated guess. You do this every single day so don't let this concept scare you. Look for the context clues, make sure they support your claim, and you'll be able to make accurate inferences and conclusions!

Reading Comprehension

Meaning From Context

Often in Reading Comprehension questions, you are asked for the definition of a word, which you have to infer from the surrounding text, called "meaning in context." Here are a few examples with step-by-step solutions, and a few tips and tricks to answering meaning from context questions.

There are thousands of words in the English language. It is impossible for us to know what every single one of them means, but we also don't have time to Google a definition every time we read a word we don't understand! Even the smartest person in the world comes across words they don't know, but luckily we can use context clues to help us determine what things actually mean.

Context clues are really just little hints that can help us determine the meaning of words or phrases and honestly, the easiest way to learn how to use context clues is to practice!

Let's start with a few basic examples.

> In some countries many people are not given access to schools, teachers, or books. In these countries, people might be illiterate.

You might not know what the word illiterate means, but let's use the clues in the sentence to help us. If people are not given access to schools, teachers, or books, what might happen? They probably don't learn what we learned in school so they might not know some of the things that we learned from our teachers! Illiterate actually means "unable to read or write." This makes sense based on the context clues!

Let's work through another example.

> We have so much technology today! So much technology that many people have started using tablets and computers to read ebooks instead of paper books! In fact, some of these people actually think that reading paper books is archaic!

Let's look for the context clues. Well, what do we know from this paragraph? We have a lot of technology and sometimes people read ebooks instead of paper books. From this we can draw the conclusion that ebooks are beginning to replace paper books because ebooks are newer and better. So if ebooks are newer and better, it must mean that paper books are older. Archaic actually means "very old or old-fashioned," which again we determined from the context clues.

Let's see if you can try a few on your own now.

Cody noticed the strawberries in his refrigerator were old and moldy, so he abstained and threw them away. What does abstained most likely mean?

    a. chose not to consume

    b. washed

    c. shared

    d. cut into pieces

The correct answer here is A. The context clues told you the strawberries were old and moldy, and that Cody did something and then threw them away. If the strawberries were moldy, and Cody abstained, it makes sense that he didn't eat them—which is choice A.

You may have chosen choice B. If the strawberries were old and moldy, Cody could have washed them. But use ALL of the context clues. After he abstained, he threw them away. Why would Cody wash them and then throw them away? That doesn't make sense! In addition, why would he share them if they were old and moldy? Finally, I suppose Cody could have cut them into pieces, but why would he need to do that before throwing them away? It doesn't make as much sense, so choice A is the correct answer!

Let's do one more.

Reading Comprehension

Scott had disdain for Lily ever since she lied to their boss and got him fired.

- a. Compassion
- b. Hate
- c. Remorse
- d. Money

The correct answer is B. Scott was fired because Lily lied. Can you imagine if this happened to you? I think you would have some pretty strong feelings just like Scott!

By understanding the context, you can determine the meaning of even the hardest of words!

POINT OF VIEW AND PURPOSE

You may not think so, but everything you read was written for a purpose. Now, it might not be the most exciting purpose, but regardless of whether it's a website, a magazine article, a book, or even a Facebook status—everything is written for a particular purpose. By understanding that purpose and the author's point of view, we can better comprehend what we read!

To determine the purpose of a written piece, you are asking yourself a very easy question. Why was this written? Usually the answer will be one of these three choices:

1. To inform
2. To persuade
3. To entertain.

First, you should ask yourself if the piece is fiction or nonfiction. Fiction is a type of writing that is not true. It is imaginary, made-up, or theoretical. For example, Harry Potter is fiction. While reading, it may seem like this world of wizards exists, but in reality, there is no Hogwarts or Diagon Alley. It is imaginary. Can you guess which purpose fiction has? Correct, choice 3—to entertain! So if you can tell if a piece is fiction or non-fiction, you can begin to narrow down the author's purpose!

Now, if a piece is non-fiction you are left with choice 1 or 2. To inform or to persuade. Here's another trick. If the piece is simply giving you INFORMation, the author's purpose is most likely to inform you! Think of an example of an informational piece you've read recently. Textbooks, most newspaper articles, how-to blogs, the instruction manual for your new cell phone, all these are great examples where the author's purpose was to inform you.

Some nonfiction pieces, though, are written to persuade you—meaning they are trying to convince you to do something or believe something. Can you think of a few examples where the author's purpose was to persuade?

When an author's purpose is to persuade you, they will have a point of view. What side is the author on? What are they trying to convince you to believe or do? Understanding a point of view will help you better understand the author's purpose.

Let's try a few examples. Determine what the author's purpose is for each of the following:

1. A packet that explains how to use an Xbox One

2. A story where a student plays Xbox One every day and becomes the youngest person to invent an Xbox One game.

3. An article that discusses the dangers of Xbox One and says nobody should ever play.

All three of these examples have similar information—Xbox One. However, the author has a different purpose in each.

Number 1 is simply to inform. It is giving you INFORMation. Number 2 is to entertain. It is a fiction story based on imagination, not facts. Number 3 is to persuade—the author is trying to convince readers that Xbox One is bad and people should stop playing.

Reading Comprehension

Now that we have a better understanding of purpose, let's dive into point of view a little deeper. Read the passage below and answer the questions.

> Mac computers are better than PC Computers. Mac computers are more expensive, but they are worth every penny. They are made better than PC computers and typically last longer. They have better software programs and almost never get viruses or break down. PC computers have to be fixed or replaced all the time and it ends being more expensive than just buying a Mac computer in the first place! Plus, Mac computers are more user friendly and they will sync with your Ipad and Iphone! I highly suggest getting a Mac if you are looking to buy a new computer.

What was the author's purpose when they wrote this paragraph?

    a. Inform

    b. Persuade

    c. Entertain

Right, you should have chosen B, to persuade. The author has an opinion, which suggests they are persuading you to do something.

What is the author's point of view?

    a. PC Computers are the best computers to buy

    b. Both Mac's and PC's are great computers if you take care of them

    c. Mac Computers are better than PC Computers

    d. Everybody should own tablets rather than computers

The correct answer is C. The author clearly thinks that Mac computers are better than PC's. This is their point of view, or what side of the argument they are on! By understanding the author's purpose and point of view, you can better understand what you read. Just remember, everything was written for a purpose! Once you understand that purpose, you can better comprehend what point the author is trying to make!

MATHEMATICS

THIS SECTION CONTAINS A SELF-ASSESSMENT AND MATH TUTORIALS. The tutorials are designed to familiarize general principles and the self-assessment contains general questions similar to the math questions likely to be on the PERT exam, but are not intended to be identical to the exam questions. The tutorials are not designed to be a complete math course, and it is assumed that students have some familiarity with math. If you do not understand parts of the tutorial, or find the tutorial difficult, it is recommended that you seek out additional instruction.

Tour of the PERT Mathematics Content

Below is a list of the likely mathematics topics likely to appear on the PERT. Make sure that you understand these topics.

Basic Mathematics

- Algebra

- Simple geometry and measurement

- Operations with polynomials

- Solving Inequalities

- Linear equations with one and two variables

- Solving quadratics

- Coordinate geometry

The questions in the self-assessment are not the same as you will find on the PERT - that would be too easy! And nobody knows what the questions will be and they change all the time. Mostly, the changes consist of substituting new questions for old, but the changes also can be new question formats or styles, changes to the number of questions in each section, changes to the time limits for each section, and combining sections. So, while the format and exact wording of the questions may differ slightly, and changes from year to year, if you can answer the questions below, you will have no problem with the mathematics section of the PERT.

Mathematics Self-Assessment

The purpose of the self-assessment is:

- Identify your strengths and weaknesses.

- Develop your personalized study plan (above)

- Get accustomed to the PERT format

- Extra practice – the self-assessments are almost a full 3rd practice test!

- Provide a baseline score for preparing your study schedule.

Since this is a Self-assessment, and depending on how confident you are with mathematics, timing yourself is optional.

Once complete, use the table below to assess your understanding of the content, and prepare your study schedule described in chapter 1.

80% - 100%	Excellent – you have mastered the content
60 – 79%	Good. You have a working knowledge. Even though you can just pass this section, you may want to review the tutorials and do some extra practice to see if you can improve your mark.
40% - 59%	Below Average. You do not understand the content. Review the tutorials, and retake this quiz again in a few days, before proceeding to the practice test questions.
Less than 40%	Poor. You have a very limited understanding. Please review the tutorials, and retake this quiz again in a few days, before proceeding to the practice test questions.

Mathematics Self-Assessment Answer Sheet

	A	B	C	D
1	○	○	○	○
2	○	○	○	○
3	○	○	○	○
4	○	○	○	○
5	○	○	○	○
6	○	○	○	○
7	○	○	○	○
8	○	○	○	○
9	○	○	○	○
10	○	○	○	○
11	○	○	○	○
12	○	○	○	○
13	○	○	○	○
14	○	○	○	○
15	○	○	○	○
16	○	○	○	○
17	○	○	○	○
18	○	○	○	○
19	○	○	○	○
20	○	○	○	○

Mathematics Self-Assessment

1. **Express in 3^4 standard form**

    a. 81
    b. 27
    c. 12
    d. 9

2. **Simplify $4^3 + 2^4$**

    a. 45
    b. 108
    c. 80
    d. 48

3. **If $x = 2$ and $y = 5$, solve $xy^3 - x^3$**

    a. 240
    b. 258
    c. 248
    d. 242

4. **$X^3 \times X^2 =$**

    a. 5^x
    b. x^{-5}
    c. x^{-1}
    d. X^5

Reading Comprehension

5. Express 100000⁰ in standard form.

   a. 1
   b. 0
   c. 100000
   d. 1000

6. Solve the linear equation: -x - 7 = -3x - 9

   a. -1
   b. 0
   c. 1
   d. 2

7. Solve the system: 4x - y = 5   x + 2y = 8

   a. (3,2)
   b. (3,3)
   c. (2,3)
   d. (2,2)

8. Add -3x² + 2x + 6 and -x² - x - 1.

   a. -2x² + x + 5
   b. -4x² + x + 5
   c. -2x² + 3x + 5
   d. -4x² + 3x + 5

9. Simplify the following expression:

3x³ + 2x² + 5x - 7 + 4x² - 5x + 2 - 3x³

   a. 6x² - 9
   b. 6x² - 5
   c. 6x² - 10x - 5
   d. 6x² + 10x - 9

10. Multiply x - 1 and $x^2 + x + 2$.

   a. $x^3 + x - 2$
   b. $x^2 + x - 2$
   c. $x^3 + x^2 - 2$
   d. $x^3 + 2x^2 - 2$

11. Factor the polynomial $9x^2 - 6x + 12$.

   a. $3(x^2 - 2x + 9)$
   b. $3(3x^2 - 3x + 4)$
   c. $9(x^2 - 3x + 3)$
   d. $3(3x^2 - 2x + 4)$

12. Find 2 numbers that sum to 21 and the sum of the squares is 261.

   a. 14 and 7
   b. 15 and 6
   c. 16 and 5
   d. 17 and 4

13. Using the factoring method, solve the quadratic equation: $x^2 + 4x + 4 = 0$

   a. 0 and 1
   b. 1 and 2
   c. 2
   d. -2

14. Using the quadratic formula, solve the quadratic equation: $x - 31/x = 0$

   a. $-\sqrt{13}$ and $\sqrt{13}$
   b. $-\sqrt{31}$ and $\sqrt{31}$
   c. $-\sqrt{31}$ and $2\sqrt{31}$
   d. $-\sqrt{3}$ and $\sqrt{3}$

Mathematics

15. Using the factoring method, solve the quadratic equation: $2x^2 - 3x = 0$

    a. 0 and 1.5
    b. 1.5 and 2
    c. 2 and 2.5
    d. 0 and 2

16. Using the quadratic formula, solve the quadratic equation: $x^2 - 9x + 14 = 0$

    a. 2 and 7
    b. -2 and 7
    c. -7 and -2
    d. -7 and 2

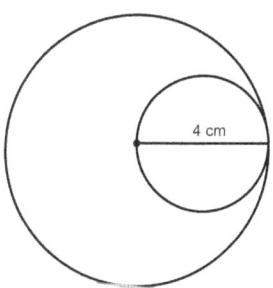

Note: figure not drawn to scale

17. Assuming the diameter of the small circle is the radius of the large circle, what is (area of large circle) - (area of small circle) in the figure above?

    a. 8 π cm²
    b. 10 π cm²
    c. 12 π cm²
    d. 16 π cm²

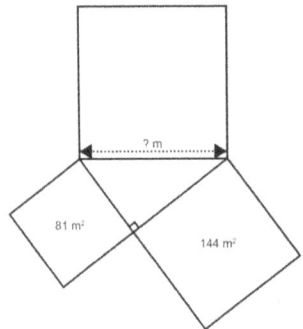

Note: figure not drawn to scale

18. Assuming the shapes around the right triangle are squares, what is the length of each side of the square above?

    a. 10
    b. 15
    c. 20
    d. 5

19. Solve the inequality: -7x - 1 ≥ 13

    a. (2, + ∞)
    b. (7, + ∞)
    c. (-∞, -2]
    d. (2, + ∞)

20. Solve the inequality: 2x - 1 ≥ x + 10

    a. (-∞, 9)
    b. (9, +∞)
    c. (-∞, -9)
    d. [11, +∞)

Answer Key

1. A

3 x 3 x 3 x 3 = 81

2. C

(4 x 4 x 4) + (2 x 2 x 2 x 2) = 64 + 16 = 80

3. D

$2(5)^3 - (2)^3 = 2(125) - 8 = 250 - 8 = 242$

4. D

$X^3 \times X^2 = X^{3+2} = X^5$

To multiply exponents with like bases, add the exponents.

5. A

Any value (except 0) raised to the power of 0 equals 1.

6. A

Collect similar terms on the same side. Here, we can collect x terms on left side, and the constants on the right:

- x - 7 = - 3x - 9 .... Let us add 3x to both sides:

- x - 7 + 3x = - 3x - 9 + 3x

2x - 7 = - 9 ... Now, we can add + 7 to both sides:

2x - 7 + 7 = - 9 + 7

2x = - 2 ... Dividing both sides by 2 gives us the value of x:

x = -2/2

x = -1

7. C

First, we need to write two equations separately:
4x - y = 5 (I)

x + 2y = 8 (II) ... Here, we can use two ways to solve the system. One is substitution method, the other one is linear elimination method:

1. Substitution Method:

Equation (I) gives us that $y = 4x - 5$. We insert this value of y into equation (II):

$x + 2(4x - 5) = 8$

$x + 8x - 10 = 8$

$9x - 10 = 8$

$9x = 18$

$x = 2$

Bu knowing $x = 2$, we can find the value of y by inserting $x = 2$ into either of the equations. Let us choose equation (I):

$4(2) - y = 5$

$8 - y = 5$

$8 - 5 = y$

$y = 3$ → solution is (2, 3)

2. Linear Elimination Method:

2•/ $4x - y = 5$ ... by multiplying equation (I) by 2, we see that -2y will form; and y terms

$\quad x + 2y = 8$ ... will be eliminated when summed with +2y in equation (II):

2•/ $4x - y = 5$

+ $\quad x + 2y = 8$
_____

$\quad 8x - 2y = 10$

+ $\quad x + 2y = 8$ ... Summing side-by-side:

$8x + x - 2y + 2y = 10 + 8$ ... -2y and +2y eliminate each other:

$9x = 18$

$x = 2$

By knowing x = 2, we can find the value of y by inserting x = 2 into either of the equations. Let us choose equation (I):

4(2) - y = 5

8 - y = 5

8 - 5 = y

y = 3 → solution is (2, 3)

8. B
$(-3x^2 + 2x + 6) + (-x^2 - x - 1)$

$= -3x^2 + 2x + 6 - x^2 - x - 1$ ... we write similar terms together:

$= -3x^2 - x^2 + 2x - x + 6 - 1$ ... we operate within the same terms:

$= -4x^2 + x + 5$

9. B
$3x^3 + 2x^2 + 5x - 7 + 4x^2 - 5x + 2 - 3x^3$ ... we write similar terms together:
$= 3x^3 - 3x^3 + 2x^2 + 4x^2 + 5x - 5x - 7 + 2$ ... we operate within the same terms. $3x^3$ and $-3x^3$, $5x$ and $-5x$ cancel:

$= 6x^2 - 5$

10. A
We are asked to multiply $(x - 1)(x^2 + x + 2)$.
Each term in the parenthesis $(x - 1)$ should be multiplied to each term in the parenthesis $(x^2 + x + 2)$:

$= x(x^2 + x + 2) - 1(x^2 + x + 2) = x^3 + x^2 + 2x - x^2 - x - 2$ ... we write similar terms together:

$= x^3 + x^2 - x^2 + 2x - x - 2$ ... we operate within the same terms. x^2 and $-x^2$ cancel:

$= x^3 + x - 2$

11. D
First, we need to search for a constant common factor in each of the terms. If there is any, we need to take it out of the equation and write it as a coefficient in front:
$9x^2 - 6x + 12 = 3(3x^2 - 2x + 4)$

We cannot go further from this point, so this is the factored form of the polynomial.

12. B

There are two statements made. This means that we can write two equations according to these statements:
The sum of two numbers are 21: $x + y = 21$

The sum of the squares is 261: $x^2 + y^2 = 261$

We are asked to find x and y.

Since we have the sums of the numbers and the sums of their squares; we can use the square formula of $x + y$, that is:

$(x + y)^2 = x^2 + 2xy + y^2$ ... Here, we can insert the known values $x + y$ and $x^2 + y^2$:

$(21)^2 = 261 + 2xy$ ... Arranging to find xy:

$441 = 261 + 2xy$

$441 - 261 = 2xy$

$180 = 2xy$

$xy = 180/2$

$xy = 90$

We need to find two number which multiply to 90. Checking the answer choices, we see that in (b), 15 and 6 are given. 15 * 6 = 90. Also their squares sum up to 261 ($15^2 + 6^2 = 225 + 36 = 261$). So these two numbers satisfy the equation.

13. D

-2
$x^2 + 4x + 4 = 0$ ... We try to separate the middle term 4x to find common factors with x^2 and 4 separately:

$x^2 + 2x + 2x + 4 = 0$ ... Here, we see that x is a common factor for x^2 and 2x, and 2 is a common factor for 2x and 4:

$x(x + 2) + 2(x + 2) = 0$ ... Here, we have x times x + 2 and 2 times x + 2 summed up. This means that we have x + 2 times x + 2:

$(x + 2)(x + 2) = 0$

$(x + 2)^2 = 0$ ... This is true if only if $x + 2$ is equal to zero.

$x + 2 = 0$

$x = -2$

14. B

To solve the equation, first we need to arrange it to appear in the form $ax^2 + bx + c = 0$ by removing the denominator:

$x - 31/x = 0$ ... First, we enlarge the equation by x:

$x * x - 31 * x/x = 0$

$x^2 - 31 = 0$

The quadratic formula to find the roots of a quadratic equation is:

$x_{1,2} = (-b \pm \sqrt{\Delta}) / 2a$ where $\Delta = b^2 - 4ac$ and is called the discriminant of the quadratic equation.

In our question, the equation is $x^2 - 31 = 0$. By remembering the form $ax^2 + bx + c = 0$:

$a = 1, b = 0, c = -31$

So, we can find the discriminant first, and then the roots of the equation:

$\Delta = b^2 - 4ac = 0^2 - 4 * 1 * (-31) = 124$

$x_{1,2} = (-b \pm \sqrt{\Delta}) / 2a = (\pm\sqrt{124}) / 2 = (\pm\sqrt{4} * 31) / 2 = (\pm 2\sqrt{31}) / 2$ ... Simplifying by 2:

$x_{1,2} = \pm\sqrt{31}$ ... This means that the roots are $\sqrt{31}$ and $-\sqrt{31}$.

15. A

$2x^2 - 3x = 0$ ... we see that both of the terms contain x; so we can take it out as a factor:

$x(2x - 3) = 0$ ... two terms are multiplied and the result is zero. This means that either of the terms or both of the terms can be equal to zero:

$x = 0$ ... this is one solution

$2x - 3 = 0 \rightarrow 2x = 3 \rightarrow x = 3/2 \rightarrow x = 1.5$ ... this is the second solution.

So, the solutions are 0 and 1.5.

16. A
To solve the equation, we need the equation in the form $ax^2 + bx + c = 0$.

$x^2 - 9x + 14 = 0$ is already in this form.

The quadratic formula to find the roots of a quadratic equation is:

$x_{1,2} = (-b \pm \sqrt{\Delta}) / 2a$ where $\Delta = b^2 - 4ac$ and is called the discriminant of the quadratic equation.

In our question, the equation is $x^2 - 9x + 14 = 0$. By remembering the form $ax^2 + bx + c = 0$:

$a = 1, b = -9, c = 14$

So, we can find the discriminant first, and then the roots of the equation:

$\Delta = b^2 - 4ac = (-9)^2 - 4 * 1 * 14 = 81 - 56 = 25$

$x_{1,2} = (-b \pm \sqrt{\Delta}) / 2a = (-(-9) \pm \sqrt{25}) / 2 = (9 \pm 5) / 2$

This means that the roots are,

$x_1 = (9 - 5) / 2 = 2$ and $x_2 = (9 + 5) / 2 = 7$

17. C
In the figure, we are given a large circle and a small circle inside it; with the diameter equal to the radius of the large one. The diameter of the small circle is 4 cm. This means that its radius is 2 cm. Since the diameter of the small circle is the radius of the large circle, the radius of the large circle is 4 cm. The area of a circle is calculated by: πr^2 where r is the radius.

Area of the small circle: $\pi(2)^2 = 4\pi$

Area of the large circle: $\pi(4)^2 = 16\pi$

The difference area is found by:

Area of the large circle - Area of the small circle = 16π - 4π = 12π

18. B
We see that there are three squares forming a right triangle in the middle. Two of the squares have the areas 81 m² and 144 m². If we denote their sides a and b respectively:

$a^2 = 81$ and $b^2 = 144$. The length which is asked is the hypotenuse; a and b are the opposite and adjacent sides of the right angle. By using the Pythagorean Theorem, we can find the value of the asked side:

Pythagorean Theorem:
(Hypotenuse)² = (Perpendicular)² + (Base)²
$h^2 = a^2 + b^2$

$a^2 = 81$, $b^2 = 144$
$h^2 = a^2 + b^2$
$h^2 = 81+144$
$h^2 = 225$
$h = 15$

19. C (-∞, -2)
To solve an inequality, we aim to leave x alone; without factors on one side, and the other numbers on the other side of the inequality sign:

$-7x - 1 \geq 13$ ... first, we add 1 to both sides:

$-7x - 1 + 1 \geq 13 + 1$

$-7x \geq 14$ ... second, we divide both sides by 7:

$-7x/7 \geq 14/7$

$-x \geq 2$ ... last, we multiply both sides by -1 to obtain a positive x. It is important not to forget that if we divide or multiply an inequality by a negative number, the inequality changes its direction:

$x \leq -2$ ... This is the solution. This means that x can be equal to -2 or a smaller value. So, (-∞, -2] is the solution.

20. D
$2x - 1 \geq x + 10$ ... first, we need to collect similar terms in the same side:

$2x - x - 1 \geq 10$

$x - 1 \geq 10$

$x \geq 10 + 1$

$x \geq 11$ ... this means that x can be 11 or a higher value; there is no upper limit for x, but lower limit is 11; including 11. This is shown as $[11, +\infty)$.

Mathematics

SOLVING ONE-VARIABLE LINEAR EQUATIONS

Linear equations with variable x is an equation with the following form:
$$ax = b$$

where a and b are real numbers. If a=0 and b is different from 0, then the equation has no solution.

Let's solve one simple example of a linear equation with one variable:
$$4x - 2 = 2x + 6$$

When we are given this type of equation, we are always moving variables to the one side, and real numbers to the other side of the equals sign. Always remember: if you are changing sides, you are changing signs. Let's move all variables to the left, and real number to the right side:

$4x - 2 = 2x + 6$
$4x - 2x = 6 + 2$
$2x = 8$
$x = 8/2$
$x = 4$

When 2x goes to the left it becomes -2x, and -2 goes to the right and becomes +2. After calculations, we find that x is 4, which is a solution of our linear equation.

Let's solve a little more complex linear equation:

$2x - 6/4 + 4 = x$
$2x - 6 + 16 = 4x$
$2x - 4x = -16 + 6$
$-2x = -10$
$x = -10/-2$
$x = 5$

We multiply whole equation by 4, to lose the fractional line. Now we have a simple linear equation. If we change sides, we change the signs.

Solving Two-Variable Linear Equations

If we have 2 or more linear equations with 2 or more variables, then we have a system of linear equations. The idea here is to express one variable using the other in one equation, and then use it in the second equation, so we get a linear equation with one variable. Here is an example:
x - y = 3
2x + y = 9

From the first equation, we express y using x.

y = x - 3

In the second equation, we write x - 3 instead of y. And there we get a linear equation with one variable x.

2x + x - 3 = 9
3x = 9 + 3
3x = 12
x = 12/3
x = 4

Now that we found x, we can use it to find y.

y = x - 3
y = 4 - 3
y = 1

So, the solution of this system is (x,y) = (4,1).

Let's solve one more system using a different method:

Solve:

5x - 3y = 17
x + 3y = 11

5x - 3y + x + 3y = 17 - 11

Notice that we have -3y in the first equation and +3y in the second. If we add these 2, we get zero, which means we lose variable y. So, we add these 2 equations and we get a linear equation with one variable.

6x = 6
x = 1

Now that we have x, we use it to find y.

5 - 3y = 17
-3y = 17 - 5
-3y = 12
y = 12/(-3)
y = -4

Adding and Subtracting Polynomials

When we are adding or subtracting 2 or more polynomials, we have to first group the same variables (arguments) that have the same degrees and then add or subtract them. For example, if we have ax^3 in one polynomial (where a is some real number), we have to group it with bx^3 from the other polynomial (where b is also some real number). Here is one example with adding polynomials:

$(-x^2 + 2x + 3) + (2x^2 + 4x - 5) =$
$-x^2 + 2x + 3 + 2x^2 + 4x - 5 =$
$x^2 + 6x - 2$

We remove the brackets, and since we have a plus in front of every bracket, the signs in the polynomials don't change. We group variables with the same degrees. We have -1 + 2, which is 1 and that's how we got x^2. For the first degree, where we have 2 + 4 which is 6, and the constants (real numbers) where we have 3 - 5 which is -2.

The principle is the same with subtracting, only we have to keep in mind that a minus in front of the polynomial changes all signs in that polynomial. Here is one example:

$(4x^3 - x^2 + 3) - (-3x^2 - 10) =$

$4x^3 - x^2 + 3 + 3x^2 + 10 =$
$4x^3 + 2x^2 + 13$

We remove the brackets, and since we have a minus in front of the second polynomial, all signs in that polynomial change. We have -3 x 2 and with minus in front, it becomes a plus and same goes for -10.

Now we group the variables with same degrees: there is no variable with the third degree in the second polynomial, so we just write 4 x 3. We group other variables the same way as adding polynomials.

MULTIPLYING AND DIVIDING POLYNOMIALS

If we have two polynomials that we need to multiply, then multiply each member of the first polynomial with each member of the second. Let's see in one example how this works:

$(x-1)(x-2) = x^2 - 2x - x + 2 = x^2 - 3x + 2$

The first member of the first polynomial is multiplied with the first member of the second polynomial and then with the second member of the second polynomial. Continue the process with the second member of the first polynomial, then simplify.

To multiply more polynomials, multiply the first 2, then multiply that result with next polynomial and so on. Here is one example:

$(1 - x)(2 - x)(3 - x) = (2 - x - 2x + x^2)(3-x)$
$= (2 - 3x + x^2)(3 - x)$
$= 6 - 2x - 9x + 3x^2 + 3x^2 - x^3 = 6 - 11x + 6x^2 - x^3$

Simplifying Polynomials

Let's say we are given some expression with one or more variables, where we have to add, subtract and multiply polynomials. We do the calculations with variables and constants and then we group the variables with the appropriate degrees. As a result, we would get a polynomial. This process is called simplifying polynomials, where we go from a complex expression to a simple polynomial.

Example:

Simplify the following expression and arrange the degrees from bigger to smaller:

$4 + 3x - 2x^2 + 5x + 6x^3 - 2x^2 + 1 = 6x^3 - 4x^2 + 8x + 5$

We can have more complex expressions such as:

$(x + 5)(1 - x) - (2x - 2) = x - x^2 + 5 - 5x - 2x + 2 = -x^2 - 6x + 7$

Here, first we multiply the polynomials and then we subtract the result and the third polynomial.

Factoring Polynomials

If we have a polynomial that we want to write as multiplication of a real number and a polynomial or as a multiplication of 2 or more polynomials, then we are dealing with factoring polynomials.

Let's see an example for a simple factoring:

$12x^2 + 6x - 4 =$
$2 * 6x^2 + 2 * 3x - 2 * 2 =$
$2(6x^2 + 3x - 2)$

We look at every polynomial member as a product of a real number and a variable. Notice that all real numbers in the polynomial are even, so they have the same number (factor). We pull out that 2 in front of the polynomial, and we write what is left.

What if have a more complex case, where we can't find a factor that is a real number? Here is an example:

$x^2 - 2x + 1 =$
$x^2 - x - x + 1 =$
$x(x - 1) - (x - 1) =$
$(x - 1)(x - 1)$

We can write -2x as –x-x. Now we group first 2 members and we see that they have the same factor x, which we can pull in front of them. For the other 2 members, we pull the minus in front of them, so we can get the same binomial that we got with the first 2 members. Now we have that this binomial is the factor for x(x - 1) and (x - 1).

If we pull x - 1 in front (underlined), from the first member we are left with x, and from the second we have -1.
And that is how we transform a polynomial into a product of 2 polynomials (in this case binomials).

QUADRATIC EQUATIONS

A. Factoring

Quadratic equations are usually called second degree equations, which mean that the second degree is the highest degree of the variable that can be found in the quadratic equation. The form of these equations is:

$ax^2 + bx + c = 0$

where a, b and c are some real numbers.

One way for solving quadratic equations is the factoring method, where we transform the quadratic equation into a product of 2 or more polynomials. Let's see how that works in one simple example:

$x^2 + 2x = 0$
$x(x + 2) = 0$
$(x = 0) \lor (x + 2 = 0)$
$(x = 0 \lor (x + -2)$

Notice that here we don't have parameter c, but this is still a quadratic equation, because we have the second degree of variable x. Our factor here is x, which we put in front, and are left with x+2. The equation is equal to 0, so either x or x+2 are 0, or both are 0.
So, our 2 solutions are 0 and -2.

B. Quadratic formula

If we are unsure how to rewrite quadratic equations so we can solve it using factoring method, we can use the formula for quadratic equation:

$$x_{1,2} = \frac{-b \pm \sqrt{b^2 - 4ac}}{2a}$$

We write $x_{1,2}$ because it represents 2 solutions of the equation. Here is one example:

$3x^2 - 10x + 3 = 0$

$x_{1,2} = \frac{-b \pm \sqrt{b^2 - 4ac}}{2a}$

$x_{1,2} = \frac{-(-10) \pm \sqrt{(-10)^2 - 4 \cdot 3 \cdot 3}}{2 \cdot 3}$

$x_{1,2} = \frac{10 \pm \sqrt{100 - 36}}{6}$

$x_{1,2} = \frac{10 \pm \sqrt{64}}{6}$

$x_{1,2} = \frac{10 \pm 8}{6}$

$x_1 = \frac{10+8}{6} = \frac{18}{6} = 3$

$x_2 = \frac{10-8}{6} = \frac{2}{6} = \frac{1}{3}$

We see that a is 3, b is -10 and c is 3.
We use these numbers in the equation and do some calculations.

Notice that we have + and -, so x_1 is for + and x_2 is for -, and that's how we get 2 solutions.

Cartesian Plane, Coordinate Plane and Coordinate Grid

To locate dots and draw lines and curves, we use the coordinate plane. It also called Cartesian coordinate plane. It is a two-dimensional surface with a coordinate grid in it, which helps us to count the units. For the counting of those units, we use x-axis (horizontal scale) and y-axis (vertical scale).

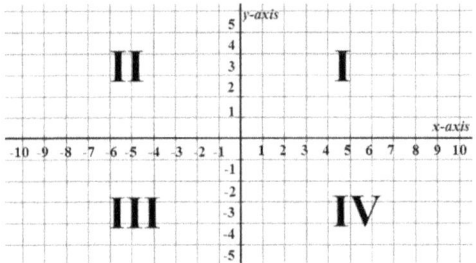

The whole system is called a coordinate system which is divided into 4 parts, called quadrants. The quadrant where all numbers are positive is the 1st quadrant (I), and if we go counterclockwise, we mark all 4 quadrants.

The location of a dot in the coordinate system is represented by coordinates. Coordinates are represented as a pair of numbers, where the 1st number is located on the x-axis and the 2nd number is located on the y-axis. So, if a dot A has coordinates a and b, then we write:

A=(a,b)   or   A(a,b)

The point where x-axis and y-axis intersect is called an origin. The origin is the point from which we measure the distance along the x and y axes.

In the Cartesian coordinate system we can calculate the distance between 2 given points. If we have dots with coordinates:
A = (a,b)

B = (c,d)

Then the distance d between A and B can be calculated by the following formula:

$$d = \sqrt{(c-a)^2 + (d-b)^2}$$

Cartesian coordinate system is used for the drawing of 2-dimentional shapes, and is also commonly used for functions.

Example:

Draw the function y = (1 - x)/2

To draw a linear function, we need at least 2 points.
If we put that x=0 then value for y would be:

$$y = \frac{1-x}{2} = \frac{1-0}{2} = \frac{1}{2}$$

We found the 1st point, let's name it A, with following coordinates:

A = (0,1/2)

To find the 2nd point, we can put that x=1. Here, the value for y would be:

$$y = \frac{1-x}{2} = \frac{1-1}{2} = \frac{0}{2} = 0$$

If we denote the 2nd point with B, then the coordinates for this point are:

B = (1,0)

Since we have 2 points necessary for the function, we find them in the coordinate system and we connect them with a line that represents the function,

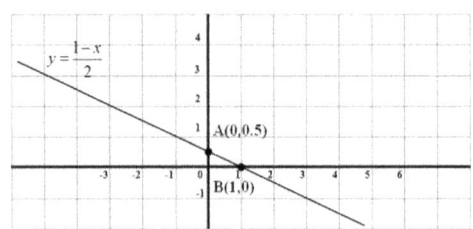

Perimeter Area and Volume

Perimeter and Area (2-dimentional shapes)

Perimeter of a shape determines the length around that shape, while the area includes the space inside the shape.

Rectangle:

P = 2a + 2b
A = ab

Square

P = 4a
A = a²

Parallelogram

P = 2a + 2b
A = ah$_a$ = bh$_b$

Mathematics

Rhombus

P = 4a
A = ah = $d_1 d_2 / 2$

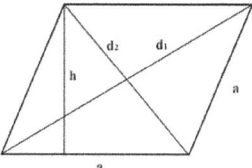

Triangle

P = a + b + c
A = $ah_a/2$ = $bh_b/2$ = $ch_c/2$

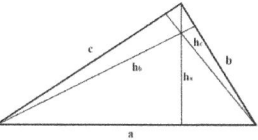

Equilateral Triangle

P = 3a
A = $(a^2 \sqrt{3})/4$

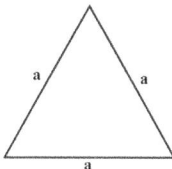

Trapezoid

P = a + b + c + d
A = ((a + b)/2)h

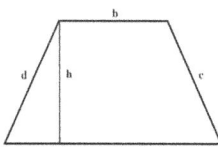

Circle

P = 2r Π
A = r^2 Π

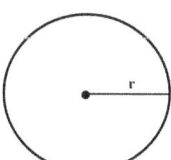

Area and Volume (3-dimentional Shapes)

To calculate the area of a 3-dimentional shape, we calculate the areas of all sides and then we add them all.

To find the volume of a 3-dimentional shape, we multiply the area of the base (B) and the height (H) of the 3-dimentional shape.

$$V = BH$$

In case of a pyramid and a cone, the volume would be divided by 3.

$$V = BH/3$$

Here are some of the 3-dimentional shapes with formulas for their area and volume:

Cuboids

A = 2(ab + bc + ac)
V = abc

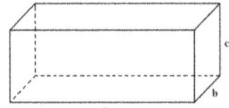

Cube

A = 6a²
V = a³

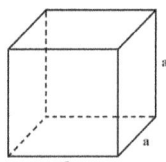

Pyramid

A = ab + ah$_a$ + bh$_b$

V = abH/3

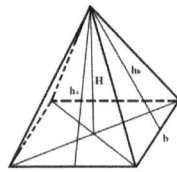

Mathematics

Cylinder

$A = 2r^2 \Pi + 2r\Pi H$
$V = r^2 \Pi H$

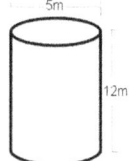

Cone

$A = (r + s)r\Pi$
$V = (r^2 \Pi H)/3$

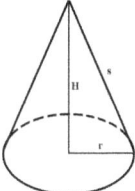

PYTHAGOREAN GEOMETRY

If we have a right triangle ABC, where its sides (legs) are a and b and c is a hypotenuse (the side opposite the right angle), then we can establish a relationship between these sides using the following formula:

$c^2 = a^2 + b^2$

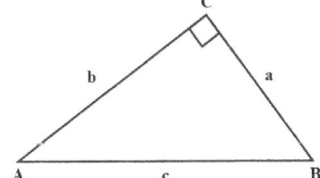

This formula is proven in the Pythagorean Theorem. There are many proofs of this theorem, but we'll look at just one geometrical proof:

If we draw squares on the right triangle's sides, then the area of the square upon the hypotenuse is equal to the sum of the areas of the squares that are upon other two sides of the triangle. Since the areas of these squares are a^2, b^2 and c^2, that is how we got the formula above.

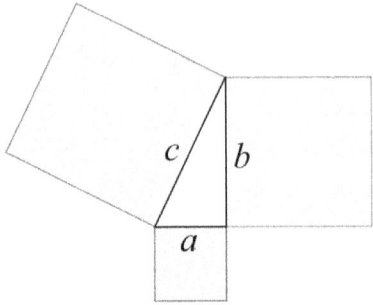

One of the famous right triangles is one with sides 3, 4 and 5. And we can see here that:

$3^2 + 4^2 = 5^2$
$9 + 16 = 25$
$25 = 25$

Example Problem:

The isosceles triangle ABC has a perimeter of 18 centimeters, and the difference between its base and legs is 3 centimeters. Find the height of this triangle.

We write the information we have about triangle ABC and draw a picture for a better understanding of the relationship

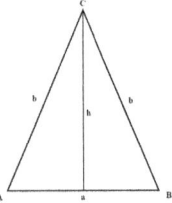

between its elements:

P=18 cm
a - b = 3 cm
h=?

We use the formula for the perimeter of the isosceles triangle, since that is what is given to us:

P=a+2b=18 cm

Notice that we have 2 equations with 2 variables, so we can solve it as a system of equations:

a + 2b = 18
a − b = 3 / a + 2b = 18
2a − 2b = 6 / a + 2b + 2a − 2b = 18 + 6
3a = 24
a = 24/3 = 8 cm

Now we go back to find b:
a − b = 3
8 − b = 3
b = 8 − 3
b = 5 cm

Using Pythagorean Theorem, we can find the height using a and b, because the height falls on the side a at the right angle. Notice that height cuts side a exactly in half, and that's why we use in the formula a/2. Here, b is our hypotenuse, so we have:

$b^2 = (a/2)^2 + h^2$
$h^2 = b^2 - (a/2)^2$
$h^2 = 5^2 - (8/2)^2$
$h^2 = 5^2 - (8/2)^2$
$h^2 = 25 - 4^2$
$h^2 = 26 - 16$
$h^2 = 9$
h = 3 cm.

QUADRILATERALS

Quadrilaterals are 2-dimentional geometrical shapes that have 4 sides and 4 angles. There are many types of quadrilaterals, depending on the length of its sides and if they are parallel and also depending on the size of its angles. All quadrilaterals have the following properties:

Sum of all interior angles is 360°

Sum of all exterior angles is 360°

A quadrilateral is a parallelogram is it fulfills at least one of the following conditions:

> Angles on each side are supplementary
> Opposite angles are equal
> Opposite sides are equal
> Diagonals intersect each other exactly in half

Here are some of the quadrilaterals:

Square

All sides are equal
All angles are right angles

Rectangle

2 pairs of equal sides
All angles are right angles

Parallelogram

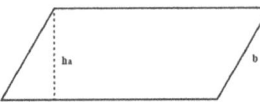

2 pairs of equal sides
Opposite angles are equal

Rhombus

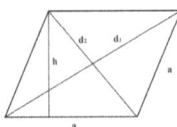

All sides are equal
Opposite angles are equal

Trapezoid

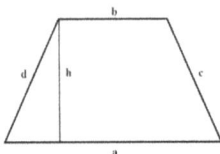

One pair of parallel sides

Example Problem
Find all angles of a parallelogram if one angle is greater than the other one by 40°.

First, we draw an image of a parallelogram:

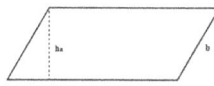

We denote angles by α and β, Since this is a parallelogram, the opposite angles are equal.

We are given that one angle is greater than the other one by 40°, so we can write:

β = α + 40°

We solve this problem in two ways:
1) The sum of all internal angles of every quadrilateral is 360°. There are 2 α and 2 β. So we have:
2α + 2β = 360°

Now, instead of β we write α + 40:
2 α + 2 (α + 40°) =360°
2 α + 2 α + 80° = 360°
4 α = 360° - 80°
4 α = 280°
α = 280° / 4
α = 70°
Now we can find β from α:
β = α + 40°
β = 70° + 40°
β = 110°

2) One of the conditions for parallelogram is " Angles on each side are supplementary" and we can use that to find these angles:
α + β = 180°
α + α + 40° = 180°

$2α = 180° - 40°$
$2α = 140°$
$α = 70°$

Now we find β:
$β = α + 40°$
$β = 70° + 40°$
$β = 110°$

WRITING

This section contains a self-assessment and writing skills tutorials. The tutorials are designed to familiarize general principles and the self-assessment contains general questions similar to the writing skills questions likely to be on the PERT exam, but are not intended to be identical to the exam questions. The tutorials are not designed to be a complete course, and it is assumed that students have some familiarity with writing skills. If you do not understand parts of the tutorial, or find the tutorial difficult, it is recommended that you seek out additional instruction.

Tour of the PERT Writing Content

The PERT writing skills section has 20 questions. Below is a list of the likely writing skills topics likely to appear on the PERT. Make sure that you understand these topics at the very minimum.

- English grammar

English usage

- Punctuation

- Subject - verb agreement

- Sentence structure

The questions in the self-assessment are not the same as you will find on the PERT - that would be too easy! And nobody knows what the questions will be and they change all the time. Mostly, the changes consist of substituting new questions for old, but the changes also can be new question formats or styles, changes to the number of questions in each section, changes to the time limits for each section, and combining sections. So, while the format and exact wording of the questions may differ slightly, and changes from year to year, if you can answer the questions below, you will have no problem with the writing skills section of the PERT.

Writing Self-Assessment

The purpose of the self-assessment is:

- Identify your strengths and weaknesses.
- Develop your personalized study plan (above)
- Get accustomed to the PERT format
- Extra practice – the self-assessments are almost a full 3rd practice test!
- Provide a baseline score for preparing your study schedule.

Since this is a Self-assessment, and depending on how confident you are with writing skills, timing yourself is optional. The PERT has 20 questions. This self-assessment has 25 questions, so allow about 20 minutes to complete.

Once complete, use the table below to assess your understanding of the content, and prepare your study schedule described in chapter 1.

80% - 100%	Excellent – you have mastered the content
60 – 79%	Good. You have a working knowledge. Even though you can just pass this section, you may want to review the tutorials and do some extra practice to see if you can improve your mark.
40% - 59%	Below Average. You do not understand the content. Review the tutorials, and retake this quiz again in a few days, before proceeding to the practice test questions.
Less than 40%	Poor. You have a very limited understanding. Please review the tutorials, and retake this quiz again in a few days, before proceeding to the practice test questions.

WRITING

	A	B	C	D	E		A	B	C	D	E
1	○	○	○	○	○	21	○	○	○	○	○
2	○	○	○	○	○	22	○	○	○	○	○
3	○	○	○	○	○	23	○	○	○	○	○
4	○	○	○	○	○	24	○	○	○	○	○
5	○	○	○	○	○	25	○	○	○	○	○
6	○	○	○	○	○						
7	○	○	○	○	○						
8	○	○	○	○	○						
9	○	○	○	○	○						
10	○	○	○	○	○						
11	○	○	○	○	○						
12	○	○	○	○	○						
13	○	○	○	○	○						
14	○	○	○	○	○						
15	○	○	○	○	○						
16	○	○	○	○	○						
17	○	○	○	○	○						
18	○	○	○	○	○						
19	○	○	○	○	○						
20	○	○	○	○	○						

Mathematics

1. Choose the sentence that is written correctly.

a. The older children have already eat their dinner, but the baby has not yet eaten anything.

b. The older children have already eaten their dinner, but the baby has not yet ate anything.

c. The older children have already eaten their dinner, but the baby has not eaten anything yet.

d. None of the sentences are correct.

2. Choose the sentence that is written correctly.

a. Its important for you to know its official name; its called the Confederate Museum.

b. It's important for you to know it's official name; it's called the Confederate Museum.

c. It's important for you to know its official name; it's called the Confederate Museum.

d. None of the sentences are correct.

3. Choose the sentence that is written correctly.

a. None of the sentences are correct.

b. If he would have known about the forecast, he would have postponed the camping trip.

c. If he have known about the forecast, he would have postponed the camping trip.

d. If he had known about the forecast, he would have postponed the camping trip.

4. Choose the sentence that is written correctly.

a. He doesn't have any money to buy clothes and neither do I.

b. He doesn't have any money to buy clothes and neither does I.

c. He don't have any money to buy clothes and neither does I.

d. None of the sentences are correct.

5. Choose the sentence that is written correctly.

a. Because it really don't matter, I don't care if I go there.

b. Because it really doesn't matter, I don't care if I go there.

c. Because it really don't matter, I don't care if I go there.

d. No change is necessary

6. Choose the sentence that is written correctly.

a. The mother would not of punished her daughter if she could have avoided it.

b. The mother would not have punished her daughter if she could of avoided it.

c. No changes are necessary.

d. The mother would not have punished her daughter if she could have avoided it.

7. Choose the sentence that is written correctly.

a. There was scarcely no food in the pantry, because nobody ate at home.

b. There was scarcely any food in the pantry, because nobody ate at home.

c. There was scarcely any food in the pantry, because not nobody ate at home.

d. No changes are necessary.

8. Choose the sentence that is written correctly.

a. Michael has lived in that house for forty years, while I has owned this one for only six weeks.

b. Michael have lived in that house for forty years, while I have owned this one for only six weeks.

c. Michael have lived in that house for forty years, while I has owned this one for only six weeks.

d. None of the sentences are correct.

9. Choose the word that best completes the sentence below.

Lee pronounced _____ name incorrectly; it's an impatiens, not an impatience.

a. it's

b. its

c. A or B

d. None of the above.

10. Choose the word that best completes the sentence below.

After the car was fixed it _____ again.

    a. None of the choices are correct.

    b. ran well

    c. would have run well

    d. ran more well

11. Choose the sentence that is written correctly..

    a. Ted and Janice, who had been friends for years, went on vacation together every summer.

    b. Ted and Janice who had been friends for years, went on vacation together every summer.

    c. Ted, and Janice who had been friends for years, went on vacation together every summer.

    d. None of the choices are correct.

12. Choose the sentence that is written correctly.

    a. None of us want to go to the party not even, if there will be live music.

    b. None of us want to go to the party, not even if there will be live music.

    c. None of us want to go to the party; not even if there will be live music.

    d. None of the choice are correct.

Writing

13. Choose the sentence that is written correctly.

a. John, Maurice, and Thomas quit school two months before graduation.

b. John, Maurice and Thomas quit school two months before graduation.

c. John Maurice and Thomas, quit school two months before graduation.

d. None of the choice are correct.

14. Choose the sentence that is written correctly.

a. "My father said that he would be there on Sunday" Lee explained.

b. None of the choices are correct.

c. "My father said that he would be there on Sunday," Lee explained.

d. "My father said that he would be there on Sunday." Lee explained.

15. Choose the sentence that is written correctly.

a. I own two dogs, a cat named Jeffrey, and Henry, the goldfish.

b. I own two dogs a cat, named Jeffrey, and Henry, the goldfish.

c. I own two dogs, a cat named Jeffrey; and Henry, the goldfish.

d. None of the choices are correct.

16. Choose the sentence below with the correct punctuation.

    a. Marcus who won the debate tournament, is the best speaker that I know.
    b. Marcus, who won the debate tournament, is the best speaker that I know.
    c. Marcus who won the debate tournament is the best speaker that I know.
    d. Marcus who won the debate tournament is the best speaker, that I know.

17. The ceremony had an emotional _____ on the groom, but the bride was not <u>affected</u>.

    a. effect
    b. affect
    c. None of the choices are correct.

18. Choose the sentence that is written correctly.

    a. None of the choices are correct.
    b. Anna was taller then Luis, but than he grew four inches in three months.
    c. Anna was taller than Luis, but than he grew four inches, in three months.
    d. Anna was taller than Luis, but then he grew four inches in three months.

19. Choose the word that best completes the sentence below.

There second home is in Boca Raton, but _____ not there for most of the year.

    a. Their
    b. There
    c. They're
    d. None of the choices are correct.

20. Choose the word that best completes the sentence below.

Their going to graduate in June; after that, their best option will be to go ____.

   a. There
   b. They're
   c. Their
   d. None of the choices are correct.

21. Choose the word that best completes the sentence below.

Your mistaken; that is not ____ book.

   a. You are
   b. Your
   c. You're
   d. None of the choices are correct.

22. Choose the word that best completes the sentence below.

You're classes are on the west side of campus, but ____ living on the east side.

   a. Your
   b. You're
   c. None of the choices are correct.

23. Choose the sentence that is written correctly.

a. The Chinese live in one of the world's most populous nations, while a citizen of Bermuda lives in one of the least populous.

b. The Chinese lives in one of the world's most populous nations, while a citizen of Bermuda live in one of the least populous.

c. The Chinese live in one of the world's most populous nations, while a citizen of Bermuda live in one of the least populous.

d. None of the choices are correct.

24. Choose the sentence that is written correctly.

a. You shouldn't sit in that chair wearing black pants; I set the white cat there just a moment ago.

b. You shouldn't set in that chair wearing black pants; I sit the white cat there just a moment ago.

c. You shouldn't set in that chair wearing black pants; I set the white cat there just a moment ago.

d. None of the choices are correct.

25. Choose the sentence that is written correctly.

a. Golden Gate Bridge in San Francisco

b. golden gate bridge in San Francisco

c. Golden gate bridge in San Francisco

d. None of the choice are correct.

Answer Key

1. C
Present perfect. You cannot use the Present Perfect with specific time expressions such as: yesterday, one year ago, last week, when I was a child, at that moment, that day, one day, etc. The Present Perfect is used with unspecific expressions such as: ever, never, once, many times, several times, before, so far, already, yet, etc.

2. C
Its vs. It's. "It's" is a contraction for it is or it has. "Its" is a possessive pronoun meaning, more or less, of it or belonging to it.

3. D
The third conditional is used for talking about an unreal situation (that did not happen) in the past. For example, "If I had studied harder, [if clause] I would have passed the exam [main clause]. Which is the same as, "I failed the exam, because I didn't study hard enough."

4. A
Disagreeing with a negative statement uses "neither."

5. B
Doesn't, does not, or does is used with the third person singular--words like he, she, and it. Don't, do not, or do is used for other subjects.

6. D
The third conditional is used for talking about an unreal situation (that did not happen) in the past. For example, "If I had studied harder, [if clause] I would have passed the exam [main clause]. Which is the same as, "I failed the exam, because I didn't study hard enough."

7. B
Double negative sentence. In double negative sentences, one of the negatives is replaced with "any."

8. D
Present perfect. You cannot use the Present Perfect with specific time expressions such as: yesterday, one year ago, last week, when I was a child, at that moment, that day, one day, etc. The Present Perfect is used with unspecific expressions such as: ever, never, once, many times, several times, before, so far, already, yet, etc.

9. B
Its vs. It's. "It's" is a contraction for it is or it has. "Its" is a possessive pronoun meaning, more or less, of it or belonging to it.

10. B
Present tense, "ran well" is correct. "Ran good" is never correct.

11. A
Use a comma to separate phrases.

12. B
Use a comma separates independent clauses. None of us wants to go to the party, not even if there will be live music.

13. B
Don't use a comma before 'and' in a list.

14. C
Commas always go with a quote and the use of said, explained etc.

15. A
This is an example if a comma which appears before 'and,' but is disambiguating. Without the comma, the sentence would be "I own two dogs, a cat named Jeffrey and Henry, the goldfish." This means there is a cat named Jeffrey and Henry, and a goldfish with no name mentioned. The comma appears to show the distinction.

I own two dogs, a cat named Jeffrey, and Henry, the goldfish.

Writing

16. B
Comma separate phrases.

17. A
Affect vs. Effect - "Affect" is a verb (action) and "effect" is a noun (thing).

18. D
Than vs. Then – Than is used for comparison, as in, taller than, and then is used for time, as in, but then...

19. C
There vs. their vs. they're. "There" indicates existence as in, "there are." "Their" indicates possession, as in, "their book." "They're" is the contraction form of "they are."

20. A
There vs. their vs. they're. "There" indicates existence as in, "there are." "Their" indicates possession, as in, "their book." "They're" is the contraction form of "they are."

21. B
Your vs. you're. "Your" is the possessive form of you. "You're" is the contraction form of you are.

22. B
Your vs. you're. "Your" is the possessive form of you. "You're" is the contraction form of you are.

23. A
Singular subjects. "The Chinese" is plural, and "a citizen of Bermuda" is singular.

24. A
Sit vs. Set. Set requires an object – something to set down. "Sit" is something that you do, like sit on the chair.

25. A
Always capitalize proper nouns.

Common English Usage Mistakes - A Quick Review

Like some parts of English grammar, usage is definitely going to be on the exam and there isn't any tricky strategies or shortcuts to help you get through this section.
Here is a quick review of common usage mistakes.

1. May and Might

'May' can act as a principal verb, which can express permission or possibility.

Examples:

Lets wait, the meeting may have started.
May I begin now?

'May' can act as an auxiliary verb, which an expresses a purpose or wish

Examples:

May you find favour in the sight of your employer.

May your wishes come true.
People go to school so that they may be educated.

The past tense of may is might.

Examples:

I asked if I might begin

'Might' can be used to signify a weak or slim possibility or polite suggestion.

Writing

Examples:

You might find him in his office, but I doubt it.
You might offer to help if you want to.

2. Lie and Lay

The verb lay should always take an object. The three forms of the verb lay are: laid, lay and laid.

The verb lie (recline) should not take any object. The three forms of the verb lie are: lay, lie and lain.

Examples:

Lay on the bed.
The tables were laid by the students.
Let the little kid lie.
The patient lay on the table.

The dog has lain there for 30 minutes.

Note: The verb lie can also mean "to tell a falsehood". This verb can appear in three forms: lied, lie, and lied. This is different from the verb lie (recline) mentioned above.

Examples:

The accused is fond of telling lies.
Did she lie?

3. Would and should

The past tense of shall is 'should', and so "should" generally follows the same principles as "shall."

The past tense of will is "would," and so "would" generally follows the same principles as "will."

The two verbs 'would and should' can be correctly used interchangeably to signify obligation. The two verbs also have some unique uses too. Should is used in three persons to signify obligation.

Examples:

I should go after work.
People should do exercises everyday.
You should be generous.

"Would" is specially used in any of the three persons, to signify willingness, determination and habitual action.

Examples:

They would go for a test run every Saturday.
They would not ignore their duties.
She would try to be punctual.

4. Principle and Auxiliary Verbs

Two principal verbs can be used along with one auxiliary verb as long as the auxiliary verb form suits the two principal verbs.

Examples:

A number of people have been employed and some promoted.

A new tree has been planted and the old has been cut down.

Again note the difference in the verb form.

5. Can and Could

A. Can is used to express capacity or ability.

Examples:

I can complete the assignment today
He can meet up with his target.

B. Can is also used to express permission.

Examples:

Yes, you can begin

In the sentence below, "can" was used to mean the same thing as "may." However, the difference is that the word "can" is used for negative or interrogative sentences, while "may" is used in affirmative sentences to express possibility.

Examples:

They may be correct.   Positive sentence - use may.
Can this statement be correct? A question using "can."
It cannot be correct. Negative sentence using "can."

The past tense of can is could. It can serve as a principal verb when it is used to express its own meaning.

Examples:

Despite the difficulty of the test, he could still perform well.

"Could" here is used to express ability.

6. Ought

The verb ought should normally be followed by the word to.

Examples:

I *ought to* close shop now.

The verb 'ought' can be used to express:

A. Desirability
You ought to wash your hands before eating. It is desirable to wash your hands.

B. Probability
She ought to be on her way back by now. She is probably on her way.

C. Moral obligation or duty
The government ought to protect the oppressed. It is the government's duty to protect the oppressed.

7. Raise and Rise

Rise
The verb rise means to go up, or to ascend.
The verb rise can appear in three forms, rose, rise, and risen. The verb should not take an object.

Examples:

The bird rose very slowly.
The trees rise above the house.
My aunt has risen in her career.

Raise
The verb raise means to increase, to lift up.
The verb raise can appear in three forms, raised, raise and raised.

Examples:

He raised his hand.
The workers requested a raise.
Do not raise that subject.

8. Past Tense and Past Participle

Pay attention to the proper use these verbs: sing, show, ring, awake, fly, flow, begin, hang and sink.

Mistakes usually occur when using the past participle and past tense of these verbs as they are often mixed up. Each of these verbs can appear in three forms:

Sing, Sang, Sung.
Show, Showed, Showed/Shown.
Ring, Rang, Rung.
Awake, awoke, awaken
Fly, Flew, Flown.
Flow, Flowed, Flowed.
Begin, Began, Begun.
Hang, Hanged, Hanged (a criminal)
Hang, Hung, Hung (a picture)
Sink, Sank, Sunk.

Examples:

The stranger rang the door bell. (simple past tense)
I have rung the door bell already. (past participle - an action completed in the past)

The stone sank in the river. (simple past tense)
The stone had already sunk. (past participle - an action completed in the past)

The meeting began at 4:00.
The meeting has begun.

9. Shall and Will

When speaking informally, the two can be used interchangeably. In formal writing, they must be used correctly.

"Will" is used in the second or third person, while "shall" is used in the first person. Both verbs are used to express a time or even in the future.

Examples:

I shall, We shall (First Person)
You will (Second Person)
They will (Third Person)

This principle however reverses when the verbs are to be used to express threats, determination, command, willingness, promise or compulsion. In these instances, will is now used in first person and shall in the second and third person.

Examples:

I will be there next week, no matter what.
This is a promise, so the first person "I" takes "will."

You shall ensure that the work is completed.
This is a command, so the second person "you" takes "shall."

I will try to make payments as promised.
This is a promise, so the first person "I" takes "will."

They shall have arrived by the end of the day.
This is a determination, so the third person "they" takes shall.

Note
A. The two verbs, shall and will should not occur twice in the same sentence when the same future is being referred to

Example:

I shall arrive early if my driver is here on time.

B. Will should not be used in the first person when questions are being asked

Examples:

Shall I go ?
Shall we go?

Subject Verb Agreement

Verbs in any sentence must agree with the subject of the sentence both in person and number. Problems usually occur when the verb doesn't correspond to the right subject or the verb fails to match the noun close to it.

Unfortunately, there is no easy way around these principals - no tricky strategy or easy rule. You just have to memorize them.

Here is a quick review:

The verb to be, present (past)

Person	Singular	Plural
First	I am (was)	we are (were)
Second	you are (were)	you are (were)
Third	he, she, it is (was)	they are (were)

The verb to have, present (past)

Person	Singular	Plural
First	I have (had)	we have (had)
Second	you have (had)	you have (had)

| Third | he, she, it has (had) | they have (had) |

Regular verbs, e.g. to walk, present (past)

Person	Singular	Plural
First	I walk (walked)	we walk (walked)
Second	you walk (walked)	you walk (walked)
Third	he, she, it walks (walked)	they work (walked)

1. Every and Each

When nouns are qualified by "every" or "each," they take a singular verb even if they are joined by 'and'

Examples:

Each mother and daughter *was* a given separate test.
Every teacher and student *was* properly welcomed.

2. Plural Nouns

Nouns like measles, tongs, trousers, riches, scissors etc. are all plural.

Examples:

The trousers *are* dirty.
My scissors *have* gone missing.
The tongs *are* on the table.

3. With and As Well

Two subjects linked by "with" or "as well" should have a verb that matches the first subject.

Examples:

The pencil, with the papers and equipment, *is* on the desk.
David as well as Louis is coming.

4. Plural Nouns

The following nouns take a singular verb:

> politics, mathematics, innings, news, advice, summons, furniture, information, poetry, machinery, vacation, scenery

Examples:

The machinery *is* difficult to assemble
The furniture *has* been delivered
The scenery *was* beautiful

5. Single Entities

A proper noun in plural form that refers to a single entity requires a singular verb. This is a complicated way of saying; some things appear to be plural, but are really singular, or some nouns refer to a collection of things but the collection is really singular.

Examples:

The United Nations Organization *is* the decision maker in the matter.

Here the "United Nations Organization" is really only one "thing" or noun, but is made up of many "nations."

The book, "The Seven Virgins" *was* not available in the library.

Here there is only one book, although the title of the book is plural.

6. Specific Amounts are always singular

A plural noun that refers to a specific amount or quantity that is considered as a whole (dozen, hundred, score etc) requires a singular verb.

Examples:

60 minutes *is* quite a long time.
Here "60 minutes" is considered a whole, and therefore one item (singular noun).

The first million is the most difficult.

7. Either, Neither and Each are always singular

The verb is always singular when used with: either, each, neither, every one and many.

Examples:

Either of the boys *is* lying.
Each of the employees *has* been well compensated
Many a police officer *has* been found to be courageous
Every one of the teachers *is* responsible

8. Linking with Either, Or, and Neither match the second subject

Two subjects linked by "either," "or," "nor" or "neither" should have a verb that matches the second subject.

Examples:

Neither David nor Paul *will* be coming.
Either Mary or Tina *is* paying.

Note
If one subject linked by "either," "or," "nor" or "neither" is in plural form, then the verb should also be in plural, and the verb should be close to the plural subject.

Examples:
Neither the mother *nor* her kids *have* eaten.
Either Mary *or* her *friends are* paying.

9. Collective Nouns are Plural

Some collective nouns such as poultry, gentry, cattle, vermin etc. are considered plural and require a plural verb.

Examples:

The *poultry are* sick.
The *cattle are* well fed.

Note
Collective nouns involving people can work with both plural and singular verbs.

Examples:

Nigerians are known to be hard working
Europeans live in Africa

10. Nouns that are Singular and Plural

Nouns like deer, sheep, swine, salmon etc. can be singular or plural and require the same verb form.

Examples:

The swine is feeding. (singular)
The swine are feeding. (plural)

The salmon is on the table. (singular)
The salmon are running upstream. (plural)

11. Collective Nouns are Singular

Collective nouns such as Army, Jury, Assembly, Committee, Team etc should carry a singular verb when they subscribe to one idea. If the ideas or views are more than one, then the verb used should be plural.

Examples:

The committee is in agreement in their decision.

The committee were in disagreement in their decision.
The jury has agreed on a verdict.
The jury were unable to agree on a verdict.

12. Subjects links by "and" are plural.

Two subjects linked by "and" always require a plural verb

Examples:

David and John are students.

Note
If the subjects linked by "and" are used as one phrase, or constitute one idea, then the verb must be singular

The color of his socks and shoe is black.
Here "socks and shoe" are two nouns, however the subject is "color" which is singular.

Punctuation

Within a sentence there are several different types of punctuation marks that can denote a pause. Each of these punctuation marks has different rules when it comes to its structure and usage, so we will look at each one in turn.

Colons

The colon is used primarily to introduce information. It can start lists such as in the sentence, "There were several things Susan had to get at the store: bread, cereal, lettuce and tomatoes." Or a colon points out specific information, such as in the sentence, "It was only then that the group fully realized what had happened: The Martian invasion had begun."

Note that if the information after the colon is a complete sentence, you capitalize and punctuate it exactly like you would a sentence. If, however, it does not constitute a complete sentence, you don't have to capitalize anything. ("Peering out the window Meredith saw them: zombies.")

Semicolons

Semicolons are super commas. They denote a stronger stop than a comma does, but they are still weaker than a period, not quite capable of ending a sentence. Semicolons are primarily used to separate independent clauses that are not being separated by a coordinating conjunction. ("Chris went to the store; he bought chips and salsa.") Semicolons can only do this, however, when the ideas in each clause are related. For instance, the sentence, "It's raining outside; my sister went to the movies," is not a proper usage of the semicolon since those clauses have nothing to do with each other.

Semicolons can be used in lists if one or more element in the list is itself made up of a smaller list. If you want to write a list of things you plan to bring to a picnic, and those things only include a Frisbee, a chair and some pasta salad, you would not need to use a semicolon. But if you also wanted to bring plastic knives, forks and spoons, you would need to write your sentence like this: "For our picnic I am bringing a Frisbee; a chair; plastic knives, forks and spoons; and some pasta salad."

Using semicolons like this preserves the smaller list that you have in your larger list.

Hyphens

To join words together to show that they are linked you use hyphens. The most common use of hyphens is to link together words to show that they are working together in a sentence. ("The well-known actor was eating at the table behind us.") This shows explicitly that you are using "well-known" as a single concept and not as two descriptive words in a list.

Hyphens can also be used to split a word in half if you run out of space writing on one line of a page. This is often seen in newspapers and magazines when text is justified to both sides of a page or a column. For example:

> The massive earthquake caused surpris-
>
> ingly little damage in the affected areas.

However, you can only use a hyphen in this way if you split the word between syllables. Often students think that they can use hyphens to break up words wherever they want; this is wrong. For the word "surprisingly" you

could have a hyphen between "sur" and "prisingly," "surpris" and "ingly, and between "surprising" and "ly," but nowhere else.

Finally, hyphens can be used to add prefixes to words. This happens a lot in news reports with phrases such as "pro-government troops."

Dashes and Parentheses

Both dashes and parentheses are used to set aside information into parenthetical statements; statements that can be treated as an aside. They do not need to be there for the sentence to make sense, but the information they provide is interesting enough that you feel it should be included. Parentheses are considered stronger than dashes are. (Commas can also be used to separate nonessential information from a sentence, but they are considered to be the weakest of the three.)

As the previous sentence shows, parentheses can surround entire sentences, separating them from the paragraph. Dashes, on the other hand, can separate off the last statement in a sentence. ("Calvin came home and greeted his family for the first time in days—everyone smiled.") Obviously, that last sentence could also be written using a semicolon or as two sentences. The difference is in how you want it to sound to the reader. Should these thoughts be treated as two distinct pieces? Or should everyone smiling at Calvin be part of the main sentence, just separated a bit more strongly—with a slightly longer pause—than a comma could manage?

Apostrophes

There are two primary uses of the apostrophe in English: forming contractions and forming possessive nouns.

Contractions are formed by taking two words and combining them together with an apostrophe replacing the missing letters (do not becomes don't), or by shortening an existing word (cannot becomes can't). Apostrophes can

also make contractions by attaching verbs to nouns or pronouns. ("He's going to the store.")

When making singular nouns possessive the general rule is that you add an 's to the end of singular nouns. (This is Tim's bagel.) When dealing with plural nouns that do not end with the letter –s (such as children), the rule is that you also add an 's to the end of the word. (It was the children's favorite movie.) And when dealing with plural nouns that end with the letter –s, you simply add an apostrophe. (My sisters' favorite game is tag.)

However, and this is an important "however" given the controversy it can cause, when dealing with singular words that end with the letter –s (such as circus), there are two standards for how to make them possessive—each with its own grammar books to back it up.

One standard says that you still add an 's to the end of the word. (This is the circus's biggest tent.) The other says that, since the word ends with an –s, it can only get an apostrophe. (This is the circus' biggest tent.) Some style books, such as the Chicago Manual of Style will go so far as to say that the former option is correct, but to avoid inflaming people's passions on the subject, using the latter is perfectly acceptable. The best thing to do is to find out which style the teacher or editor you are writing for at any given time prefers and conform to it for that person.

COMMAS

Commas are probably the most commonly used punctuation mark in English. Commas can break the flow of writing to give it a more natural sounding style, and they are the main punctuation mark used to separate ideas. Commas also

Writing

separate lists, introductory adverbs, introductory prepositional phrases, dates and addresses.

The most rigid way that commas are used is when separating clauses. There are two primary types of clauses in a sentence, independent and subordinate (sometimes called dependent). Independent clauses are clauses that express a complete thought, such as, "Tim went to the store." Subordinate clauses, on the other hand, only express partial thoughts that serve to expand on an independent clause such as, "after the game ended," which you can see is clearly not a complete sentence. (You will learn more about clauses in different lessons.)

The rule for commas with clauses is that a comma must separate the clauses when a subordinate clause comes first in a sentence: "After the game ended, Tim went to the store." But there should not be a comma when a subordinate clause follows an independent clause: "Tim went to the store after the game ended." If you leave the comma out of the first example, you have a run-on sentence. If you add one into the second example, you have a comma-splice error. Also, when you have two independent clauses joined together with a coordinating conjunction, you need to separate them with a comma. "Tim went to the store, and Beth went home."

There are some artistic exceptions to these rules, such as adding a pause for literary effect, but generally they are set in stone.

Commas are also used to separate items in a list. This area of English is unfortunately less clear than it should be, with two separate rules depending on what standard you are following. To understand the two different rules, let's pretend you are having a party at your house, and you are making a list of refreshments your friends will want. You may decide to serve three things: 1) pizza 2) chips 3) drinks. There are two different rules governing how you should punctuate this. According to many grammar books, you would write this as, "At the store I will buy pizza, chips, and drinks." This variation puts a comma after each item in the list. It is the version that the style books used in most college English and history courses will prefer, so it is probably the one you should follow. However, the Associated Press style guide, which is used in college journalism classes and at newspapers and magazines, says the sentence should be written like this: "At the store I will buy pizza, chips and drinks." Here you only use a comma between the first two words, letting the word "and" act as the separator between the last two.

Another important place to use commas is when you have a modifier that describes an element of a sentence, but that does not directly follow the thing it describes. Look at the sentence: "Tim went over to visit Beth, watching the full moon along the way." In this sentence there is no confusion about who is "watching the full moon"; it is Tim, probably as he walks to Beth's house. If you remove the comma, however, you get this: "Tim went over to visit Beth watching the full moon along the way." Now it sounds as though Beth is watching the full moon, and we are forced to wonder what "way" the moon is traveling along.

Commas are also used when adding introductory prepositional phrases and introductory adverbs to sentences. A comma is always needed following an introductory adverb. ("Quickly, Jody ran to the car.") Commas are even necessary when you have an adverb introducing a clause within a sentence, even if the clause not the first clause of the sentence. ("Amanda wanted to go to the movie; however, she knew her homework was more important.")

With introductory prepositional phrases you only add a comma if the phrase (or if a group of introductory phrases) is five or more words long. Thus, the sentence you just read did not have a comma following its introductory prepositional phrase ("With introductory prepositional phrases") because it was only four words. Compare that to this sentence with a five word introductory phrase: "After the ridiculously long class, the friends needed to relax."

The last main way that commas are used in sentences is to separate out information that does not need to be there. For instance, "My cousin Hector, who wore a blue hat at the party, thought you were funny." The fact that Hector wore a blue hat is interesting, but it is not vital to the sentence; it could be removed and not changed the sentence's meaning. For this reason it gets commas around it. Along these lines you should remember that any clause introduced by the word that is considered to provide essential information to the sentence and should not get commas around it. Conversely, any clause starting with the word which is considered nonessential and should not get commas around it.

Quotation Marks

Quotation marks are used in English in a variety of different ways. The most common use of quotation marks is to show quotations either as dialogue or, when directly quoting a source in an essay or news article. Fortunately, both of these uses follow the same basic rules.

When you have a quote written as the second part of a sentence, you need to put a comma before the quotation marks and a period inside the quotation marks at the end. (Franklin said, "Let's go to the store.") Conversely, when you have quote as the first part of the sentence with information describing it second, a comma replaces the period at the end of the sentence inside the quotes. ("Let's go to the store," Franklin said.)

If the information in a quote is not a complete sentence, you do not need to capitalize it or put commas around it, provided that it is not dialogue. (No one thought the idea of "going to the store" sounded very fun.)

Note that when the last word in a sentence has both a quotation mark and a period attached to it, the period is always inside the quotes. This is the case when you have a complete sentence inside a quote ("Let's go to the store."), and when the last word in a sentence just happens to have quote marks around it (Kerri said I was "mean.") You also need to do the same thing with commas. (Kerri said I was "mean," and it made me feel bad.) However, other punctuation marks such as colons, semicolons and dashes do not follow this rule and should come outside of the quotes. (Kerri said I was "mean"; it made me feel bad.)

When you want to use a quote inside a quote, you use the

standard double-quotation marks for the outer quote and single-quotation marks for the inner quote. ("The sign on the door said 'no soliciting,' so we went to the next house.")

Non-period end punctuation marks—exclamation points and question marks—will sometimes go inside the quotation marks and sometimes outside, depending on how much of the sentence they refer to. If the end punctuation refers only to what is in the quote, it goes inside the quotation marks. ("Everyone fleeing the zombie attack screamed, "Run!") Quotation marks are also used around certain types of titles. To figure out which ones, it helps to look at which titles are not put in quotes as well.

Titles are generally broken down into two categories: large works and small works. Large works are things such as newspapers, magazines, CDs, books and television shows. The defining characteristic of a large work is that it is able to hold small works in it. Small works are the articles inside newspapers and magazines, the songs on a CD, the chapters in a book and the episodes of a television show. It is small works that get quotation marks around them. (Large works, meanwhile, are either underlined or italicized.)

Using quotation marks correctly in a title looks something like this: The two-page article entitled "San Francisco Giants Win World Series" appeared in yesterday's New York Times. The article title is in quotes, and the newspaper title is in italics.

How to Answer English Grammar Multiple Choice - Verb Tense

This tutorial is designed to help you answer English Grammar multiple choice questions as well as a very quick refresher on verb tenses. It is assumed that you have some familiarity with the verb tenses covered here. If you find these questions difficulty or do not understand the tense construction, we recommend you seek out additional instruction.

Tenses Covered

1. Past Progressive
2. Present Perfect
3. Present Perfect Progressive
4. Present Progressive
5. Simple Future
6. Simple Future – "Going to" Form
7. Past Perfect Progressive
8. Future Perfect Progressive
9. Future Perfect
10. Future Progressive
11. Past Perfect

1. The Past Progressive Tense

How to Recognize This Tense

He *was running* very fast when he fell.

They *were drinking* coffee when he arrived.

About the Past Progressive Tense

This tense is used to speak of an action that was in progress in the past when another event occurred.

The action was unfolding at a point in the past.

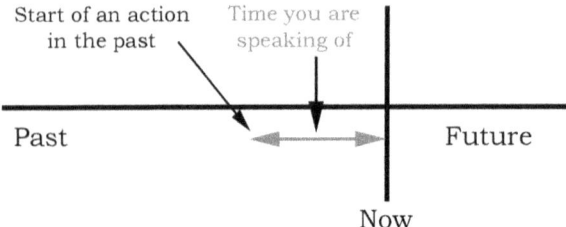

Past Progressive Tense Construction

This tense is formed by using the past tense of the verb "to be" plus the present participle of the main verb.

Sample Question

Bill _____ lunch when we arrived.

    a. will eat

    b. is eating

    c. eats

    d. was eating

How to Answer This Type of Question

1. First examine the question for clues about the time frame.

The sentence ends with "when we arrived," so we know the time frame is a point ("when") in the past (arrived).

The correct answer will refer to an ongoing action at a point of time in the past.

2. Examine the choices and eliminate any obviously incorrect answers.

Choice A is the future tense so we can eliminate.

Choice B is the present continuous so we can eliminate.

Choice C is present tense so we can eliminate.

Choice D refers to an action that takes place at a point of time in the past ("was eating").

2. The Present Perfect Tense

How to Recognize This Tense

I *have had* enough to eat.

We *have been* to Paris many times.

I *have known* him for five years.

I *have been* coming here since I was a child.

About the Present Perfect Tense

This tense expresses the idea that something happened (or didn't happen) at an unspecific time in the past until the present. The action happened at an unspecified time in the past. (If there is a specific time mentioned, the simple past tense is used.) It can be used for repeated action, accomplishments, changes over time and uncompleted action.

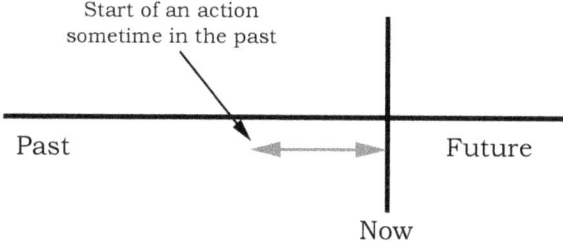

Present Perfect Tense Construction

It is also used with "for" and "since."

This tense is formed by using the present tense of the verb "to have" plus the past participle of the main verb.

Sample Question

I _____ these birds many times.

    a. am seeing

    b. will saw

    c. have seen

    d. have saw

How to Answer This Type of Question

1. First examine the question for clues about the time frame.

"Many times" tells us that the action is repeated and in the past.

2. Examine the choices and eliminate any obviously incorrect answers.

Choice A, "am seeing" is incorrect because it is a continuing action, i.e. in the present; it also doesn't use a form of 'have'.

Choice B is grammatically incorrect.

Choice C is tells of something that has happened in the past and is now over. This is the best choice so far.

Choice D is grammatically incorrect.

3. The Present Perfect Progressive Tense

How to Recognize This Tense

We *have been seeing* a lot of rainy days.

I *have been reading* some very good books.

About the Present Perfect Progressive Tense

This tense expresses the idea that something happened (or didn't happen) in the relatively recent past, but <u>the action is not finished.</u> It is used to express the duration of the action.

NOTE: The present perfect speaks of an action that happened sometime in the past, but this action is finished. In the present perfect progressive tense, the action that started in the past is still going on.

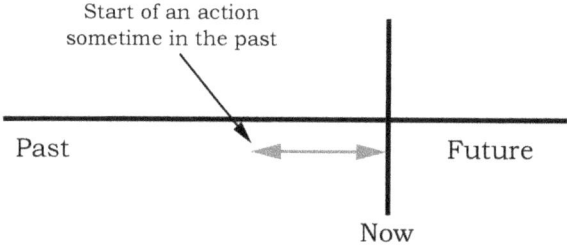

Present Perfect Progressive Tense Construction

This tense is formed by using the present tense of the verb "to have," plus "been," plus the present participle of the main verb.

Sample Question

Bill _____ there for two hours.

    a. sits

    b. sitting

    c. has been sitting

    d. will sat

How to Answer This Type of Question

1. First examine the question for clues about the time frame.

"For two hours" tells us that the action, "sits," is continuous up to now, and may continue into the future.

Note this sentence could also be the simple past tense,

Bill sat there for two hours.

Or the future tense,

Bill will sit there for two hours.

However, these are not among the choices.

2. Examine the choices and eliminate any obviously incorrect answers.

Choice A is incorrect because it is the present tense.
Choice B is incorrect because it is the present continuous.
Choice C is correct. "Has been sitting" expresses a continuous action in the past that isn't finished.
Choice D is grammatically incorrect.

4. The Present Progressive Tense

How to Recognize This Tense

We *are having* a delicious lunch.

They *are driving* much too fast.

About the Present Progressive Tense

This tense is used to express what the action is <u>right now</u>. The action started in the recent past, and is continuing into the future.

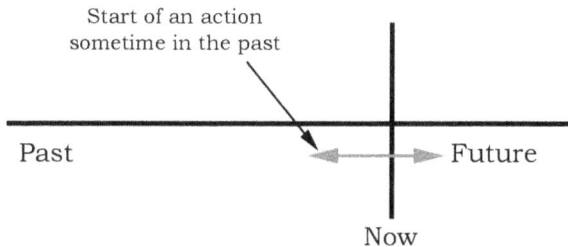

Present Perfect Tense Construction

The Present Progressive Tense is formed by using the present tense of "to be" plus the present participle of the main verb.

Sample Question

She _____ very hard these days.

    a. works

    b. is working

    c. will work

    d. worked

How to Answer This Type of Question

1. First examine the question for clues about the time frame.

The end of the sentence includes "these days" which tell us the action started in the past, continues into the present, and may continue into the future.

2. Examine the choices and eliminate any obviously incorrect answers.

Choice A, the simple present is incorrect.
Choice B, "is working" is correct.
Check the other two choices just to be sure. Choice C is future tense, and choice D is past tense, so they can be eliminated.

The correct answer is choice B.

5. The Simple Future Tense

How to Recognize This Tense

I *will see* you tomorrow.
We *will drive* the car.

About the Simple Future Tense

This tense shows that the action will happen sometime in the future.

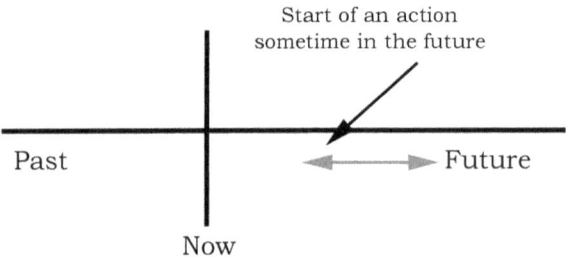

Simple Future Tense Construction

The tense is formed by using "will" plus the root form of the verb. (The root form of the verb is the infinitive without "to." Examples: read, swim.)

Sample Question

We _____ to Paris next year.

  a. went
  b. had been
  c. will go
  d. go

How to Answer This Type of Question

1. First examine the question for clues about the time frame.

The last two words of the sentence, "next year," clearly identify this sentence as referring to the future.

2. Examine the choices and eliminate any obviously incorrect answers.

Choice A is the past tense and can be eliminated.

Choice B is the past perfect tense and can be eliminated.

Choice D is the simple present and can be eliminated.

Choice C is the only one left and is the correct simple future tense.

6. The Simple Future Tense – The "Going to" Form

How to Recognize This Tense

I *am going to* see you tomorrow.

We *are going to* drive the car.

About the Simple Future Tense

This form of the future tense is used to show the intention of doing something in the future. (This is the strict grammatical meaning, but in daily speech, it is often used interchangeably with the simple future tense, the "will" form.)

The tense is formed by using the present conditional tense of "to go," plus the infinitive of the verb.

Sample Question

I _____ shopping in an hour.

    a. go

    b. have gone

    c. am going to go

    d. went

How to Answer This Type of Question

1. First examine the question for clues about the time frame.

"In an hour" clearly identifies the action as taking place in the future.

2. Examine the choices and eliminate any obviously incorrect answers.

Choice A is the simple present tense and can also be eliminated.

Choice B is the past perfect and can be eliminated.

Choice C is the correct answer.

Choice D is the past tense and can be eliminated.

7. The Past Perfect Progressive Tense

How to Recognize This Tense

I *had been sleeping* for an hour when you phoned.

We *had been eating* our dinner when they all came into the dining room.

About the Past Perfect Progressive Tense

This tense is used to show that the action had been going on for a period of time in the past when another action, also in the past, occurred.

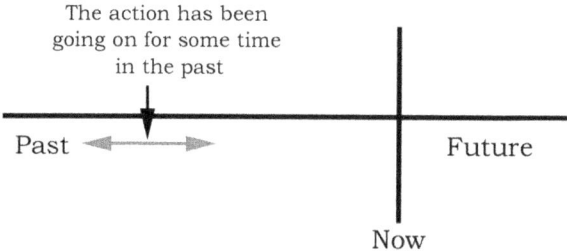

Past Perfect Tense Construction

The tense is formed by using the past perfect tense of the verb "to be" plus the present participle of the main verb.

Sample Question

How long _____ you _____ when I saw you?

    a. are _____ running

    b. had _____ running

    c. had _____ been running

    d. was _____ running

How to Answer This Type of Question

1. First examine the question for clues about the time frame.

"When I saw" tells us the sentence happened at a point of time ("when") in the past ("saw").

2. Examine the choices and eliminate any obviously incorrect answers.

Choice A, "are running" is incorrect and can be eliminated.

Choice B, "Had ___ running" is grammatically incorrect and can be eliminated.

Choice C is correct.

Choice D is grammatically incorrect so the answer is choice C.

8. Future Perfect Progressive Tense

How to Recognize This Tense

I *will have been working* here for two years in March.

I *will have been driving* for four hours when I get there, so I will be tired.

About the Future Perfect Progressive Tense

This tense is used to show that the action continues up to a point of time in the future.

Future Prefect Progressive Tense Construction

This tense is formed by using the future perfect tense of "to be" plus the present participle of the main verb.

Writing

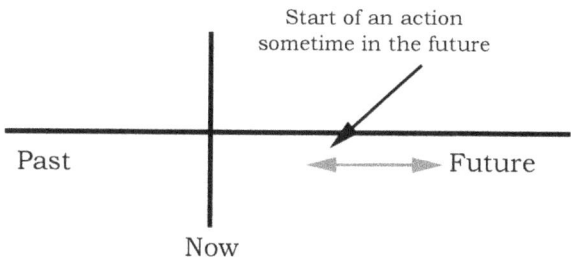

Sample Question

_____ you _____ all the time I am gone?

    a. have _____ been working

    b. will _____ have been working

    c. are _____ worked

    d. will _____ worked

How to Answer This Type of Question

1. First examine the question for clues about the time frame.

"All the time I am gone" refers to an action in the future ("time I am gone") and the action is progressive ("all the time"). The progressive action means the correct choice will be a verb tense that ends in "ing."

2. Examine the choices and eliminate any obviously incorrect answers.

Choice A, the past perfect, refers to a past continuous event and is also grammatically incorrect in the sentence, so choice A can be eliminated.

Choice B looks correct because it refers to an action will be going on for a period of time in the future.

Examine choices C and D just to be sure. Both choices are

9. The Future Perfect Tense

How to Recognize This Tense

By next November, I *will have received* my promotion.

By the time he gets home, she is going *to have cleaned* the entire house.

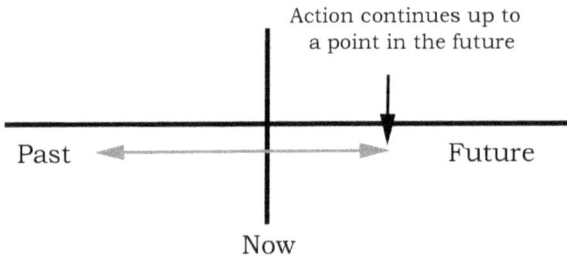

About the Future Perfect Tense

The future perfect tense expresses action in the future before another action in the future. This is the past in the future. For example:

He *will have prepared* dinner when she arrives.

Future Perfect Tense Construction

This tense is formed by "will + have + past participle."

Writing

Sample Question

They _____ their seats before the game begins.

    a. will have find

    b. will find

    c. will have found

    d. found

How to Answer This Type of Question

1. First examine the question for clues about the time frame.

This question could be several different tenses. The only clue about the time frame is "before the game begins," which refers to a specific point of time.

We know it isn't in the past, because "begins" is incorrect for the past tense. Similarly with the present. So the question is about something that happens in the future, before another event in the future.

2. Examine the choices and eliminate any obviously incorrect answers.

Choice A can be eliminated as incorrect. Choice B looks good, so mark it and check the others before making a final decision. Choice C is the past perfect and can be eliminated because the time frame is incorrect. Choice D is the simple past tense and can be eliminated for the same reason.

10. Future Progressive Tense

How to Recognize This Tense

The teams *will be playing* soccer when we arrive.

At 3:45 the soccer fans *will be waiting* for the game to start at 4:00 o'clock

At 3:45 the soccer players *will be preparing* to play at 4:00 o'clock

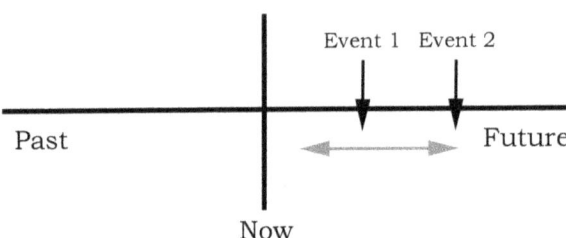

About the Future Progressive Tense

The future progressive tense talks about a continuing action in the future.

Future Progressive Tense Construction

will+ be + (root form) + ing = will be playing

Sample Question

Many excited fans _____ a bus to see the game at 4:00.

    a. catch

    b. catching

    c. have been catching

    d. will be catching

Writing

How to Answer This Type of Question

1. First examine the question for clues about the time frame.

"At 4:00," tells us the sentence is either in the past OR in the future.

2. Examine the choices and eliminate any obviously incorrect answers.

From the time frame of the sentence, the answer will be past or future tense.

Choice A is the present tense and can be eliminated. Choice B is the present continuous tense and can be eliminated. Choice C is the past perfect continuous and can be eliminated. Choice D is the only one left. Quickly examining the tense, it is future progressive and is correct in the sentence.

11. The Past Perfect Tense

How to Recognize This Tense

The party *had* just *started* when the coach arrived.

We *had waited* for twenty minutes when the bus finally came.

About the Past Perfect

The past perfect tense talks about two events that happened in the past and establishes which event happened first.

Another example is, "We had eaten when he arrived."

The two events are "eat" and "he arrived." From the sentence above the past perfect tense tells us the first event, "eat" happened before the second event, "he arrived."

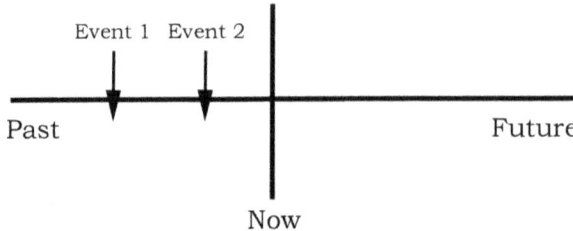

I had already eaten when my friends arrived.

Past Perfect Tense Construction

The past perfect is formed by "have" plus the past participle.

Sample Question

It was time to go home after they _____ the game.

    a. will win

    b. win

    c. had won

    d. wins

How to Answer This Type of Question

1. First examine the question for clues about the time frame.

"Was" tells us the sentence happened in the past. Also notice there are two events, "go home" and "after the game."

2. Examine the choices and eliminate any obviously incorrect answers.

Choice A is the future tense and can be eliminated. Choice B is the simple present and can be eliminated. Choice C is the past perfect and orders the two events in the past. Choice D is the present tense and incorrect and can be eliminated, so choice C is the correct answer.

How to Write an Essay

Writing an essay can be a difficult process, especially under time constraints in an exam. Here are three simple steps to help you to write a solid, well thought out essay:

1. **Brainstorm** potential themes and general ideas for your essay.

2. **Outline** your essay step by step, including subheadings for ease of understanding.

3. **Write** your essay carefully being aware of proper grammar and sentence structure.

1. Brainstorming

You should first spend some time thinking about the general subject of the essay. If the essay is asking a question, you must make sure to answer this fully in your essay. You may find it helpful to highlight key words in your assignment or use a simple spider diagram to jot down key ideas.

Example

> Read the following information and complete the following assignment:
>
> Joseph Conrad is a Polish author who lived in England for most of his life and wrote a huge amount of English literature. Much of his work was completed during the height of the British Empire's colonial imperialism.
>
> Assignment: What impact has Joseph Conrad had on modern society? Present your point of view on the matter and support it with evidence. Your evidence may include reasoning, logic, examples from readings, your own experience, and observations.

Joseph Conrad

> **Background?** sailor, adventure, Polish immigrant, Youth, Nostromo, Heart of Darkness
> **Themes in his works?** ivory, silver trading, colonialism, corruption, greed
> **Thoughts?** descent into madness, nature of evil

2. Outlining or Planning

An outline or plan is critical to organize your thoughts and ideas fully and logically. There are many ways to do this; the easiest is to write down the following headings:

1. Title
2. Introduction
3. Body
4. Conclusion

You should then jot down key ideas and themes that fit logically under the appropriate heading. This plan is now the backbone of your essay.

Tip: Even if you are not required to produce an outline or plan for the assignment, you should always leave it with your essay in the exam booklet or the back of the assignment paper. Simply draw a line across it and write 'plan' or 'outline'. This demonstrates to the reader the approach you use in formulating and finally writing your essay.

3. WRITING THE ESSAY

Your introduction is what will help the reader to decide whether they want to read the rest of your essay. The introduction also introduces the subject matter and allows you to provide a general background to the reader. The first sentence is very important and you should avoid starting the essay with openers such as 'I will be comparing…'

Example

>Born as Józef Teodor Konrad Korzeniowski on December 3rd, 1857, Joseph Conrad led an adventurous life. As a Polish immigrant, Conrad never quite fit into England where he spent most of his adult life. As a younger man, Conrad made a living off sailing voyages. These swashbuckling experiences soon had him writing tales of the high seas such as one of his first works, Youth. While his early, adventurous work was of high quality, Conrad is best remembered for shedding light on the exploitative side of colonialism. Age and experience led him to start writing about (and challenging) the darker side of the

imperial way of thinking. Conrad's work has forever soured words such as colonialism and imperialism.

In the main part, or body of your essay, you should always be yourself and be original.

- Avoid using clichés.
- Be aware of your tone.
- Consider the language that you use. Avoid jargon and slang. Use clear prose and imagery.
- Your writing should always flow; remember to use transitions, especially between paragraphs. Read aloud in your head to make sure a paragraph sounds right.
- Always try to use a new paragraph for new ideas.

Example

Conrad's written fiction focused on themes such as greed and power. He portrayed these two concepts as purveyors of evil. Greed and power may take on different guises, but the end result would always be the same.

Perhaps his most famous piece, The Heart of Darkness, is about the descent of an English ivory trader, Mr. Kurtz, into madness. We are taken up a river resembling the Congo by a narrator, Marlow, who is sent to retrieve Mr. Kurtz. Marlow eventually finds that Kurtz has been diluted by power and greed, the two things that spurred on colonialism in Africa. Kurtz has taken charge of a large tribe of natives (that he brutalizes) and has been hoarding ivory for himself.

Much of Conrad's later work was cut from the same vein as The Heart of Darkness. His crowning achievement is considered Nostromo where he takes an idealistic hero and corrupts him with colonial greed. Only this time the greed is for silver, not ivory.

> Conrad's work resonates with readers partly because it was semi-autobiographical. Where his experience sailing the high seas helped bring his adventure stories to light, likewise did his experience witnessing atrocities in Africa reverberate through his writing.

The conclusion is your last chance to impress your reader and brings your entire essay to a logical close. You may want to link your conclusion back to your introduction or provide some closing statements. Do not panic if you cannot close your essay off completely. Few subjects offer closure.

Your conclusion should always be consistent with the rest of the essay and you should never introduce a new idea in your conclusion. It is also important to remember that a weak conclusion can diminish the impact of a good essay.

Example

> In sum, Joseph Conrad's life experiences and masterful writing left a lasting impact on the image of progress and what it meant to "move forward." He brought to light the cost in human lives that was required for Europe to continue mining natural resources from foreign lands. Joseph Conrad had a permanent impact on imperial culture, and colonial brutality has been on the decline ever since his work was published.

Presentation

Poor grammar and punctuation can ruin an otherwise good essay. You should always follow any requirements about the presentation of your essay, such as word count. You should also make sure that your writing is legible. Always allow time for one final read-through before submission.

Tip: If you are able to, write with double spacing. If you make a mistake, you can cross it out and write the correction on the blank line above.

Some final points to think about for writing a solid, well thought out essay:

- A good essay will contain a strong focus.

- There is no set essay structure but you can use sub-headings for better readability.

- Avoid particularly sensitive or controversial material. If you must write about something controversial, always make sure to include counter arguments.

- Your essay may have little to do with the subject itself; it is about what you make of the subject.

- Your essay can include examples from your readings, experience, studies or observations.

- Spend time doing practice essays and looking at sample essays beforehand.

ANOTHER EXAMPLE

Here is another example using the three steps required to write a good essay:

1. **Brainstorming**
2. **Outlining**
3. **Writing**

Using a second essay, we can now explore these three steps in further detail.

1. BRAINSTORMING

Example

> Think about the information that follows, and the assignment below.
>
> People often quote the last two lines of Robert Frost's "The Road not Taken" as being metaphorical for success. The line's read "I took

the one less traveled by, / And that has made all the difference" (19, 20).

Assignment: Analyze and interpret this poem. Consider the poem's place in Modernist culture and Robert Frost's personal experiences. Read between the lines and identify the more complex aspects/themes of this poem. Outline and complete an essay that challenges the point of view presented above, that the poem is synonymous with success. Provide evidence backed up by logic, experience, research, and/ or examples from the poem.

The assignment and key words that appear in the brief above are being highlighted. This confirms that the essay is not asking a specific question, but instead, it is asking for discussion of the subject matter and phrases.
This is the time to take a few moments to jot down initial thoughts about the assignment. Do not worry too much about proper grammar at this point, just get all your thoughts down on paper:

"The Road Not Taken" by Robert Frost

> **Background?** Modernist poetry
> **Themes?** Life decisions, regret, fate, the unknown future
> **Thoughts?** The diverging roads are symbolic, the sigh at end signifies regret, life has many twists and turns, you can end in a drastically different situation later after a simple decision now

2. OUTLINING OR PLANNING

Outlining or planning is the next important stage in the process and you should always spend a few minutes writing a plan. This plan is just as important as the essay itself. You can also note how much **time** you may want to spend on a particular section. Make sure to assign headings to each main section of the essay and include important questions/themes you want to address.

Example

   1. Title

   2. Essay introduction
   Identify and discuss the underlying theme/s in Robert Frost's "The Road Not Taken"
   What was Frost's background and its applicability to understanding this poem?

   3. Essay body
   Quick summary of the poem
   Discuss key themes and other concepts
   Discuss how these things relate to Modernism

   4. Essay conclusion
   Rephrase the themes of Robert Frost's poem and their place in modernist doctrine

This plan is now the outline for the essay.

3. WRITING

The introduction is important, as it needs to introduce the reader to the essay in a way that will encourage them to continue reading. A good introduction will introduce the subject matter to a reader and point out relevant information that may be helpful to know when reading the rest of the essay.

Example

   Identify and discuss the underlying theme/s in Robert Frost's "The Road Not Taken"

   Robert Frost wrote during the artistic movement after World War I known as Modernism. One purpose of modernism was to remake things in a new light, to analyze and change symptoms of societies that had plunged the European world into a grisly war. Frost's poem, "The Road Not Taken," carries with it a burden of regret that was a staple of Modernist art.

This introduction opens with what explaining about the time period of Robert Frost and real life influences to the theme of his poem, "The Road Not Taken." It contains some powerful language that will encourage the reader to continue reading and gives a solid base in understanding the remainder of the essay.

The main part or **body of the essay** is also very important:

Example

>"The Road Not Taken" was almost assuredly influenced by Robert Frost's personal life. He was very familiar with facing difficult decisions. Frost had to make the decision to send both his sister and daughter to mental institutions. His son Carol committed suicide at the age of 38. The list of loss Frost experienced in his life goes on, but it suffices to say he was familiar with questioning the past.
>
>With no other hints of the narrator's identity, it is best to assume that he is a man similar to Frost himself. The poem itself is about a nameless narrator reflecting on when he traveled through the autumn woods one day. He had come across a split in the road and expresses regret that he could not travel both. Each road is described as looking similar and as having equal wear but it is also mentioned one was grassier. The roads were unknown to the narrator, and shared equal possibilities in how well they may or may not be around their bends. He tells his listener with a sigh that he had made his decision and had taken "the road less traveled by" (19). Even though he had little idea which road would be better in the long run, the one he chose proved difficult.
>
>This poem is a collection of all the insecurities and possibilities that come with even the simplest decisions. We experience the sorrow expressed by the narrator in the opening

> lines with every decision we make. For all the choices you make in life, there is a counterweight of choices you have not made. In a way, we are all missing half of our lives' possibilities. This realization causes a mixture of regret and nostalgia, but also stokes in us the keen awareness that missed opportunities are inevitable and regretting them is a waste of energy. We often find ourselves stuck, as the narrator is, between questioning the decisions we've made and knowing that this natural process isn't exactly productive.
>
> Unsolvable regret and nostalgia are things that the Modernists fought with on a regular basis. They often experimented in taking happenings of the past and reinventing them to fit a new future.

The body of the essay opens with providing a brief overview of Robert Frost's personal life and his life's relevance to the over-arching theme of dealing with difficult decisions in the poem, "The Road Not Taken."

A new paragraph starts where appropriate and at the end of the discussion of Robert Frost's life, a **transition** moves the reader back to the start of the book (closing off this section).

This also helps to move the reader towards the next discussion point.

The tone of this essay is formal, mainly because of the seriousness of the subject – regret and nostalgia plays a major role in people's lives all around the world.

For the conclusion, there will be a summary of the main discussion. While it is ideal for you to impress the reader with your writing, more importantly you need to make sure you cover all your bases and address the assignment appropriately with a closing statement about any important points you discussed in the body of your essay.

Example

> In conclusion, Robert Frost's poem "The Road

Not Taken" deals with themes of fate, regret, sorrow, and the many possibilities our decisions hold. Consider how easy it would be to upturn your life today if you made a few decisions you normally wouldn't. Frost's poem forces us to consider the twists and turns our lives take. Perhaps with a sigh, we could all think about the choices that for us have made all the difference.

This conclusion is consistent with the rest of the essay in terms of style. There are no new ideas introduced and it has referred to the main points in the assignment title.

Finally, a full read-through is necessary before submission. It only takes a couple of minutes to read through and pick up any errors. Remember to double space to leave room for any corrections to be made. You can also leave spacing at the end of each paragraph if you should need to add an additional sentence or two.

Common Essay Mistakes - Example 1

Whether the topic is love or action, reality television shows damage society. Viewers witness the personal struggles of strangers and they experience an outpouring of emotions in the name of entertainment. This can be dangerous on many levels. Viewers become numb to real emotions and values. Run the risk of not interpreting a dangerous situation correctly. 1 The reality show participant is also at risk because they are completely exposed. 2 The damage to both viewers and participants leads to the destruction of our healthy societal values.

Romance reality shows are dangerous to the participants and contribute to the emotional problems witnessed in society today as we set up a system built on equality and respect, shows like "The Bachelor" tear it down. 3 In front of millions of viewers every week, young women compete for a man. Twenty-five women claim to be in love with a man they just met. The man is reduced to an object they compete for. There are tears, fights, and manipulation aimed at winning the prize. 4 Imagine a young woman's reality when she returns home and faces the scrutiny of viewers who watched her unravel on television every Monday night. These women objectify themselves and have learned 5 that relationships are a combination of hysteria and competition. This does not give hope to a society based on family values and equality.

6 While incorporating the same manipulations and breakdown of relationships offered on "The Bachelor," shows like "Survivor" add another level of danger. Not only are they building a society based on lying to each other, they are competing in physical challenges that become dangerous. In the name of entertainment, these challenges become increasingly physical and are usually held in a hostile environment. The viewer's ability to determine the safety of an activity is messed up. 7 To entertain and preserve their pride, participants continue in competitions regardless of the danger level. For example, 8 participants on "Survivor" have sustained serious injuries as heart attack and burns. Societal rules are based on the safety of its citizens, not on hurting yourself for entertainment.

Reality shows of all kinds are dangerous to participants. They damage society. 9

1. Correct sentence fragments. Who/what runs the risk? Add a subject or combine sentences. Try: "Viewers become numb to real emotions and run the risk of not interpreting a dangerous situation correctly."

2. Correct redundant phrases. Try: "The reality show participant is also at risk because they are exposed."

3. Correct run-on sentences. Decide which thoughts should be separated. Try: "Romance reality shows are dangerous to participants and contribute to the emotional problems of society today. As we support a system built on equality and respect, shows like "The Bachelor" tear it down."

4. Vary sentence structure and length. Try: "Twenty-five women claim to be in love with a man who is reduced to being the object of competition. There are tears, fights, and manipulation aimed at winning the prize."

5. Use active voice. Try: These women objectify themselves and learned that relationships are a combination of hysteria and competition.

6. Use transitions to tie paragraphs together. Try: Start the paragraph with, "Action oriented reality shows are equally as dangerous to the participants."

7. Avoid casual language/slang. Try: "The viewer's ability to determine the safety of an activity is compromised."

8. Don't address the essay. Avoid phrases like "for example" and "in conclusion." Try: "Participants on "Survivor" have sustained serious injuries as heart attack and burns.

9. Leave yourself time to write a strong conclusion! Try: Designate 3-5 minutes for writing your conclusion.

Common Essay Mistakes - Example 2

Questioning authority makes society stronger. In every aspect our society, there is an authoritative person or group making rules. There is also the group underneath them who are meant to follow. 1 This is true of our country's public schools as well as our federal government. The right to question authority at both of these levels is guaranteed by the United States Declaration of Independence. People are given the ability to question so that authority figures are kept in check 2 and will be forced to listen to the opinions of other people. Questioning authority leads to positive changes in society and preserves what is already working well.

If students never question the authority of a principal's decisions, the best interest of the student body is lost. Good things 3 may not remain in place for the students and no amendment to the rules are sought. Change requires that authority be questioned. For example, that Silver Head Middle School in Davie, Florida. Last year, the principal felt strongly about enforcing the school's uniform policy. Some students were not bothered by this. 4 Many students felt the policy disregarded their civil rights. A petition voicing student dissatisfaction was signed and presented to the principal. He met with a student representative to discuss the petition. Compromise was reached as a monthly "casual day." The students were able to promote change and peace by questioning authority.

Even at the level of federal government, our country's ultimate authority, the ability to question is the key to the harmony keeping society strong. Most government officials are elected by the public so they have the right to question their authority. 5 If there's a mandate, law, or statement that citizens aren't 6 happy with, they have recourse. Campaigning for, or against a political platform and participating in the electoral process give a voice to every opinion. I think elections are very important. 7 Without this questioning and examination of society's laws, the government will represent only the voice of the authority figure. The success of our society is based on the questioning of authority. 8
     Society is strengthened by those who question authority. Dialogue is created between people with different visions and change becomes possible. At both the level of public school and of federal government, the positive effects of questioning authority can be witnessed. Whether questioning the decisions of a single principal or the motives of the federal government, it is the willingness of people to question and create change that allows society to grow. A strong society is inspired by many voices, all at different levels. 9 These voices keep society strong.

1. Write concisely. Combine the sentences to improve understanding and cut unnecessary words. Try: "In every aspect of society, there is an authority making rules and a group of people meant to follow them."

2. Avoid slang. Re-word "kept in check." Try: "People are given the ability to question so that authority figures are held accountable and will be forced to listen to the opinions of other people.

2-2. Cut unnecessary words. Try: "People are given the ability to question so that authority figures are held accountable and will listen to other opinions."

3. Use precise language. What are "good things?" Try: "Interesting activities may not remain in place for the students and no amendment to the rules are sought."

Use correct subject-verb agreement. Be careful to identify the correct subject of your sentence. Try: "Interesting activities may not remain in place for the students and no amendment to the rules is sought."

4. Don't add information that doesn't add value to your argument. Cut: "Some students weren't bothered by this."

5. Check for parallel structure. Who has the right to question whose authority? Try: "Having voted them in, the people have the authority to question public officials."

6. Don't use contractions in academic essays. Try: "If there is a mandate, law, or statement that citizens are not happy with, they have recourse."

7. Don't use the pronoun "I" in persuasive essays. Cut opinions. Cut:"I think elections are very important."

8. Use specific examples to prove your argument. Try: Discuss a particular election in depth.

9. Cut redundant sentences. Cut: "A strong society is inspired by many voices, all at different levels."

Writing Concisely

Concise writing is direct and descriptive. The reader follows the writer's thoughts easily. If your writing is concise, a four paragraph essay is acceptable for standardized tests. It's better to write clearly about fewer ideas than to write poorly about many.

This doesn't always mean using fewer words. It means that every word you use is important to the message. Unnecessary or repetitive information dilutes ideas and weakens your writing. The meaning of the word concise comes from the Latin, "to cut up." If it isn't necessary information, don't waste precious testing minutes writing it down.

Being redundant is a quick way to lengthen a sentence or paragraph, but it takes away your power during a timed essay. While many writers use repetition of phrases and key words to make their point, it's important to remove words that don't add value. Redundancy can confuse and lead you away from your subject when you need to write quickly. Be aware that many redundant phrases are part of our daily language and need to be cut from your essay.

For example, "bouquet of flowers" is a redundant phrase as only the word "bouquet" is necessary. Its definition includes flowers. Be especially careful with words you use to stress a point, such as "completely," "totally," and "very."

First of all, I'd like to thank my family.
Revised: First, I'd like to thank my family.

The school *introduced a new* rule.
Revised: The school introduced a rule.

I am *completely full*.
Revised: I am full.

Your glass is *totally empty*!
Revised: Your glass is empty!

Her artwork is *very unique*.
Revised: Her artwork is unique.

Other ways to cut bulk and time include avoiding phrases that have no meaning or power in your essay. Phrases like "in my opinion," "as a matter of fact," and "due to the fact that" are space and time wasters. Also, change passive verbs to active voice.

In my opinion, the paper is well written.
Revised: The paper is well written.

The book *was written* by the best students.
Revised: The best students wrote the book.

The teacher *is listening* to the students.
The teacher listens to the students.

This assigns action to the subject, shortens, and clarifies the sentence. When time is working against you, precise language is on your side.

Not only should you remove redundant phrases, whole sentences without value should be cut too. Replacing general nouns with specific ones is an effective way to accomplish this.

She screamed as the thing came closer. It was a sharp-toothed dog.
Revised: She screamed as the sharp-toothed dog came closer.
The revised sentence is precise and the paragraph is improved by combining sentences and varying sentence structure. When editing, ask yourself which thoughts should be connected and which need to be separated. Skim each paragraph as you finish writing it and cut as you go.

Leave three to four minutes for final editing. While reading, make a point to pause at every period. This allows you to "hear" sentences the way your reader will, not how you meant them to sound. This will help you find the phrases and sentences that need to be cut or combined. The result is an essay a grader will appreciate.

Avoiding Redundancy

Duplication and verbosity in English is the use of two or more words that clearly mean the same thing, making one of them unnecessary. It is easy to do use redundant expressions or phrases in a conversation where speech is spontaneous, and common in spoken English. In written English, however, redundancy is more serious and harder to ignore. Here are list of redundant phrases to avoid.

1. Suddenly exploded.

An explosion is instantaneous or immediate and that is sudden enough. No need to use 'suddenly' along with exploded.

2. Final outcome.

An outcome refers to the result. An outcome is intrinsically final and so no need to use final along with outcome.

3. Advance notice/planning/reservations/ warning.

A warning, notice, reservation or plan is made before an event. Once the reader sees any of these words, they know that they were done or carried out before the event. These words do not need to be used with advance.

4. Began, new beginning.

Beginning signals the start or the first time, and therefore the use of "new" is superfluous.

5. Add an additional.

The word 'add' indicates the provision of another something, and so "additional" is superfluous.

6. For a period/number of days.

The word "days" is already in plural and clearly signifies more than just one day. It is thus redundant to use "a number of," or "a period of" along with days. Simply state the number of days or of the specific number of days is unknown, you say 'many days.'

7. Foreign imports.

Imports are foreign as they come from another country, so it is superfluous to refer to imports as "foreign."

8. Forever and ever.

Forever indicates eternity and so there is no need for "ever" as it simply duplicated forever.

9. Came at a time when.

"At a time" is not necessary in this phrase because the 'when' already provides a temporal reference to the action, coming.

10. Free gift.

It cannot be a gift if it is paid for. A gift, by nature, is free and so referring to a gift is free is redundant.

11. Collaborate/join/meet/merge together.

The words merge, join, meet and collaborate already suggest people or things coming together. It is unnecessary to use any of these words with together, such as saying merge together or join together. The correct expression is to simply say join or merge, omitting the together.

12. Invited guests.

Guests are those invited for an event. Since they had to be invited to be guests, there is no need to use invited with guests.

13. Major breakthrough.

A breakthrough is significant by nature. It can only be described as a breakthrough when there is a notable progress. The significant nature of the progress is already implied when you use the word "breakthrough," so "major" is redundant.

14. Absolutely certain or sure/essential/ guaranteed.

When someone or something is said to be sure or certain it indicates that it is without doubt. Using "absolutely" in addition to certain or sure is unnecessary. Essential or guaranteed is used for something that is absolute and so also does not need the word absolutely to accompany them.

15. Ask a question.

Ask means to present a question. Using "question" in addition to "ask" is redundant.

16. Basic fundamentals/essentials.

Using basic here is redundant. Essentials and fundamental suggest an elementary nature.

17. [Number] a.m. in the morning/p.m. in the evening.

When you write 8 a.m. the reader knows you mean 8 o'clock in the morning. It is not necessary to say 8 a.m. in the morning. Simply write 8 a.m. or 8 p.m.

18. Definite decision.

A decision is already definite even if it can be reversed later. A decision is a definite course of action has been chosen. No need to use the word definite along with the word decision.

19. Past history/record.

A record or history by definition refers to past events or occurrences. Using past to qualify history or record is unnecessary.

20. Consensus of opinion.

Consensus means agreement over something that may be or not be an opinion. So it may look that using the phrase 'consensus of opinion' is appropriate, but it is better to omit "opinion."

21. Enter in.

Enter means going in, as no one enters out. Therefore no need to add "in," simply use "enter."

22. Plan ahead.

You cannot plan for the past. Planning can only be done for the future. When you use "plan," the future is already implied.

23. Possibly might.

The words might and possibly signify probability, so just use one at a time.

24. Direct confrontation.

A confrontation is a head-on conflict, and does not need to be modified with "direct."

25. Postpone until later.

Something postponed is delayed or moved to a later time, and does not need to be modified with "later."

26. False pretense.

The word pretense is only used to describe a deception, so a "false" pretense is redundant.

27. Protest against.

Protest involves showing opposition; there is no need to use against.

28. End result.

Result only comes at the end. The reader who sees the word 'result' already knows that it occurs at the end.

29. Estimated at about/roughly.

Estimates are approximations that are not expected to be accurate, and do not need to be modified with "roughly" or "about."

30. Repeat again.

Repeat refers to something repeated and does not need to be modified with "again."

31. Difficult dilemma.

A dilemma is a situation that is complicated or difficult, and does not need to be modified with "difficult."

32. Revert back.

Revert indicates returning to a former or earlier state. Something that reverts goes back to how it used to be. No need to add back.

33. (During the) course (of).

During means "in or throughout the duration of," and doesn't require the use of the word "course."

34. Same identical.

Same and identical means the same thing and should not be used together.

35. Completely filled/finished/opposite.

Completely indicates thoroughness. However, the words finished and filled already indicate something thoroughly filled or finished to the extent possible. The words filled and finished thus do not need to be qualified with "completely."

36. Since the time when.

In this phrase, 'the time when' is not necessary as 'since' already indicates sometime in the past.

37. Close proximity/scrutiny.

Proximity means being close, in respect to location. Scrutiny means studying something closely. Both words suggest close, whether in respect to location as with proximity, or in respect to study, as with scrutiny. It is therefore unnecessary to use the words together.

38. Spell out in detail.

'Spell out' involves providing details, so no need to add "in detail."

39. Written down.

Anything written can be said to be taken down. Written should therefore be used on its own.

40. (Filled to) capacity.

Anything that is filled has reached its capacity and so the word capacity does not need to be used along with filled.

41. Unintended mistake.

Something is a mistake because it is not intended. The lack of intention is plain and so there is no need to qualify with "unintended."

42. Still remains.

"Remains" signifies that something is still as it is, and so using 'still' is superfluous.

43. Actual experience/fact.

Something becomes an experience after it has occurred. If it didn't occur it is not an experience. A fact can only be a fact when it is sure or confirmed. Both experience and fact thus do not need to be modified with "actual."

44. Therapeutic treatment.

Therapeutic refers to the healing or curing of illness. All medical treatment is therapeutic in that it aims to heal or cure. When speaking of medical treatment, there is thus no need to use therapeutic to qualify treatment.

45. At the present time.

"At present" alone indicates the present time or "at this time." Using "at the present time" is the verbose version. Better to just use "at present."

46. Unexpected surprise.

A surprise is unexpected by nature. The unexpected nature is assumed once the word surprised is read or heard. No need to use unexpected to qualify it.

47. As for example.

"As" indicates the use of an example and so it is redundant to say "an example."

48. Usual custom.

A custom refers to something that is observed or done repeatedly or routinely. The use of 'usual' along with custom is not necessary.

49. Added bonus.

Bonus already shows something extra, in addition to the ordinary. Using "added" to describe the bonus is not necessary.

50. Few in number.

Something is few because it is small in number. No need to use number with few.

Practice Test Questions Set 1

The questions below are not the same as you will find on the PERT - that would be too easy! And nobody knows what the questions will be and they change all the time. Below are general questions that cover the same subject areas as the PERT. So, while the format and exact wording of the questions may differ slightly, and change from year to year, if you can answer the questions below, you will have no problem with the PERT.

For the best results, take these practice test questions as if it were the real exam. Set aside time when you will not be disturbed, and a location that is quiet and free of distractions. Read the instructions carefully, read each question carefully, and answer to the best of your ability.
Use the bubble answer sheets provided. When you have completed the practice questions, check your answer against the Answer Key and read the explanation provided.

Do not attempt more than one set of practice test questions in one day. After completing the first practice test, wait two or three days before attempting the second set of questions.

Reading

	A	B	C	D	E		A	B	C	D	E
1	○	○	○	○	○	21	○	○	○	○	○
2	○	○	○	○	○	22	○	○	○	○	○
3	○	○	○	○	○	23	○	○	○	○	○
4	○	○	○	○	○	24	○	○	○	○	○
5	○	○	○	○	○	25	○	○	○	○	○
6	○	○	○	○	○	26	○	○	○	○	○
7	○	○	○	○	○	27	○	○	○	○	○
8	○	○	○	○	○	28	○	○	○	○	○
9	○	○	○	○	○	29	○	○	○	○	○
10	○	○	○	○	○	30	○	○	○	○	○
11	○	○	○	○	○						
12	○	○	○	○	○						
13	○	○	○	○	○						
14	○	○	○	○	○						
15	○	○	○	○	○						
16	○	○	○	○	○						
17	○	○	○	○	○						
18	○	○	○	○	○						
19	○	○	○	○	○						
20	○	○	○	○	○						

Mathematics

	A	B	C	D	E			A	B	C	D	E
1	○	○	○	○	○		26	○	○	○	○	○
2	○	○	○	○	○		27	○	○	○	○	○
3	○	○	○	○	○		28	○	○	○	○	○
4	○	○	○	○	○		29	○	○	○	○	○
5	○	○	○	○	○		30	○	○	○	○	○
6	○	○	○	○	○		31	○	○	○	○	○
7	○	○	○	○	○		32	○	○	○	○	○
8	○	○	○	○	○		33	○	○	○	○	○
9	○	○	○	○	○		34	○	○	○	○	○
10	○	○	○	○	○		35	○	○	○	○	○
11	○	○	○	○	○		36	○	○	○	○	○
12	○	○	○	○	○		37	○	○	○	○	○
13	○	○	○	○	○		38	○	○	○	○	○
14	○	○	○	○	○		39	○	○	○	○	○
15	○	○	○	○	○		40	○	○	○	○	○
16	○	○	○	○	○		41	○	○	○	○	○
17	○	○	○	○	○		42	○	○	○	○	○
18	○	○	○	○	○		43	○	○	○	○	○
19	○	○	○	○	○		44	○	○	○	○	○
20	○	○	○	○	○		45	○	○	○	○	○
21	○	○	○	○	○		46	○	○	○	○	○
22	○	○	○	○	○		47	○	○	○	○	○
23	○	○	○	○	○		48	○	○	○	○	○
24	○	○	○	○	○		49	○	○	○	○	○
25	○	○	○	○	○		50	○	○	○	○	○

Writing Skills

	A	B	C	D	E		A	B	C	D	E
1	○	○	○	○	○	26	○	○	○	○	○
2	○	○	○	○	○	27	○	○	○	○	○
3	○	○	○	○	○	28	○	○	○	○	○
4	○	○	○	○	○	29	○	○	○	○	○
5	○	○	○	○	○	30	○	○	○	○	○
6	○	○	○	○	○	31	○	○	○	○	○
7	○	○	○	○	○	32	○	○	○	○	○
8	○	○	○	○	○	33	○	○	○	○	○
9	○	○	○	○	○	34	○	○	○	○	○
10	○	○	○	○	○	35	○	○	○	○	○
11	○	○	○	○	○	36	○	○	○	○	○
12	○	○	○	○	○	37	○	○	○	○	○
13	○	○	○	○	○	38	○	○	○	○	○
14	○	○	○	○	○	39	○	○	○	○	○
15	○	○	○	○	○	40	○	○	○	○	○
16	○	○	○	○	○	41	○	○	○	○	○
17	○	○	○	○	○	42	○	○	○	○	○
18	○	○	○	○	○	43	○	○	○	○	○
19	○	○	○	○	○	44	○	○	○	○	○
20	○	○	○	○	○	45	○	○	○	○	○
21	○	○	○	○	○	46	○	○	○	○	○
22	○	○	○	○	○	47	○	○	○	○	○
23	○	○	○	○	○	48	○	○	○	○	○
24	○	○	○	○	○	49	○	○	○	○	○
25	○	○	○	○	○	50	○	○	○	○	○

Reading and Language Arts

Directions: The following questions are based on several reading passages. A series of questions follow each passage. Read each passage carefully, and then answer the questions based on it. You may reread the passage as often as you wish. When you have finished answering the questions based on one passage, go right onto the next passage. Choose the best answer based on the information given and implied.

Questions 1 – 4 refer to the following passage.

Passage 1 - The Life of Helen Keller

Many people have heard of Helen Keller. She is famous because she was unable to see or hear, but learned to speak and read and went onto attend college and earn a degree. Her life is a very interesting story, one that she developed into an autobiography, which was then adapted into both a stage play and a movie. How did Helen Keller overcome her disabilities to become a famous woman? Read on to find out. Helen Keller was not born blind and deaf. When she was a small baby, she had a very high fever for several days. As a result of her sudden illness, baby Helen lost her eyesight and her hearing. Because she was so young when she went deaf and blind, Helen Keller never had any recollection of being able to see or hear. Since she could not hear, she could not learn to talk. Since she could not see, it was difficult for her to move around. For the first six years of her life, her world was very still and dark.

Imagine what Helen's childhood was like. She could not hear her mother's voice. She could not see the beauty of her parent's farm. She could not recognize who was giving her a hug, or a bath or even where her bedroom was each night. Sadly, she could not communicate with her parents in any way. She could not express her feelings or tell them the things she wanted. It must have been a very sad childhood.

Practice Test Questions 1

When Helen was six years old, her parents hired her a teacher named Anne Sullivan. Anne was a young woman who was almost blind. However, she could hear and she could read Braille, so she was a perfect teacher for young Helen. At first, Anne had a very hard time teaching Helen anything. She described her first impression of Helen as a "wild thing, not a child." Helen did not like Anne at first either. She bit and hit Anne when Anne tried to teach her. However, the two of them eventually came to have a great deal of love and respect.

Anne taught Helen to hear by putting her hands on people's throats. She could feel the sounds people made. In time, Helen learned to feel what people said. Next, Anne taught Helen to read Braille, which is how books are written for the blind. Finally, Anne taught Helen to talk. Although Helen did learn to talk, it was hard for anyone but Anne to understand her.

As Helen grew older, she amazed more and more people with her story. She went to college and wrote books about her life. She gave talks to the public, with Anne at her side, translating her words. Today, both Anne Sullivan and Helen Keller are famous women who are respected for their lives' work.

1. Helen Keller could not see and hear and so, what was her biggest problem in childhood?

    a. Inability to communicate

    b. Inability to walk

    c. Inability to play

    d. Inability to eat

2. Helen learned to hear by feeling the vibrations people made when they spoke. What were these vibrations were felt through?

    a. Mouth

    b. Throat

    c. Ears

    d. Lips

3. From the passage, we can infer that Anne Sullivan was a patient teacher. We can infer this because

a. Helen hit and bit her and Anne remained her teacher.

b. Anne taught Helen to read only.

c. Anne was hard of hearing too.

d. Anne wanted to be a teacher.

4. Helen Keller learned to speak but Anne translated her words when she spoke in public. The reason Helen needed a translator was because

a. Helen spoke another language.

b. Helen's words were hard for people to understand.

c. Helen spoke very quietly.

d. Helen did not speak but only used sign language.

Questions 5 – 7 refer to the following passage.

Passage 2 - Ways Characters Communicate in Theater

Playwrights give their characters voices in a way that gives depth and added meaning to what happens on stage during their play. There are different types of speech in scripts that allow characters to talk with themselves, with other characters, and even with the audience.

It is very unique to theater that characters may talk "to themselves." When characters do this, the speech they give is called a soliloquy. Soliloquies are usually poetic, introspective, moving, and can tell audience members about the feelings, motivations, or suspicions of an individual character without that character having to reveal them to other characters on stage. "To be or not to be" is a famous soliloquy given by Hamlet as he considers difficult but important themes, such as life and death.

The most common type of communication in plays is when

one character is speaking to another or a group of other characters. This is generally called dialogue, but can also be called monologue if one character speaks without being interrupted for a long time. It is not necessarily the most important type of communication, but it is the most common because the plot of the play cannot really progress without it.

Lastly, and most unique to theater (although it has been used somewhat in film) is when a character speaks directly to the audience. This is called an aside, and scripts usually specifically direct actors to do this. Asides are usually comical, an inside joke between the character and the audience, and very short. The actor will usually face the audience when delivering them, even if it's for a moment, so the audience can recognize this move as an aside.

All three of these types of communication are important to the art of theater, and have been perfected by famous playwrights like Shakespeare. Understanding these types of communication can help an audience member grasp what is artful about the script and action of a play.

5. According to the passage, characters in plays communicate to

    a. move the plot forward

    b. show the private thoughts and feelings of one character

    c. make the audience laugh

    d. add beauty and artistry to the play

6. When Hamlet delivers "To be or not to be," he can be described as

    a. solitary

    b. thoughtful

    c. dramatic

    d. hopeless

7. The author uses parentheses to punctuate "although it has been used somewhat in film,"

    a. to show that films are less important

    b. instead of using commas so that the sentence is not interrupted

    c. because parenthesis help separate details that are not as important

    d. to show that films are not as artistic

Questions 8 – 10 refer to the following passage.

Passage 3 - Low Blood Sugar

As the name suggest, low blood sugar is low sugar levels in the bloodstream. This can occur when you have not eaten properly and undertake strenuous activity, or, when you are very hungry. When Low blood sugar occurs regularly and is ongoing, it is a medical condition called hypoglycemia. This condition can occur in diabetics and in healthy adults.

Causes of low blood sugar can include excessive alcohol consumption, metabolic problems, stomach surgery, pancreas, liver or kidneys problems, as well as a side-effect of some medications.

Symptoms

There are different symptoms depending on the severity of the case.

Mild hypoglycemia can lead to feelings of nausea and hunger. The patient may also feel nervous, jittery and have fast heart beats. Sweaty skin, clammy and cold skin are likely symptoms.
Moderate hypoglycemia can result in a short temper, confusion, nervousness, fear and blurring of vision. The patient may feel weak and unsteady.

Severe cases of hypoglycemia can lead to seizures, coma,

fainting spells, nightmares, headaches, excessive sweats and severe tiredness.

Diagnosis of low blood sugar

A doctor can diagnosis this medical condition by asking the patient questions and testing blood and urine samples. Home testing kits are available for patients to monitor blood sugar levels. It is important to see a qualified doctor though. The doctor can administer tests to ensure that will safely rule out other medical conditions that could affect blood sugar levels.

Treatment

Quick treatments include drinking or eating foods and drinks with high sugar contents. Good examples include soda, fruit juice, hard candy and raisins. Glucose energy tablets can also help. Doctors may also recommend medications and well as changes in diet and exercise routine to treat chronic low blood sugar.

8. Based on the article, which of the following is true?

    a. Low blood sugar can happen to anyone.

    b. Low blood sugar only happens to diabetics.

    c. Low blood sugar can occur even.

    d. None of the statements are true.

9. Which of the following are the author's opinion?

    a. Quick treatments include drinking or eating foods and drinks with high sugar contents.

    b. None of the statements are opinions.

    c. This condition can occur in diabetics and in healthy adults.

    d. There are different symptoms depending on the severity of the case

10. What is the author's purpose?

    a. To inform

    b. To persuade

    c. To entertain

    d. To analyze

11. Which of the following is not a detail?

    a. A doctor can diagnosis this medical condition by asking the patient questions and testing.

    b. A doctor will test blood and urine samples.

    c. Glucose energy tablets can also help.

    d. Home test kits monitor blood sugar levels.

    d. None of the above.

Questions 12 – 15 refer to the following passage.

How To Get A Good Nights Sleep

Sleep is just as essential for healthy living as water, air and food. Sleep allows the body to rest and replenish depleted energy levels. Sometimes we may for various reasons have trouble sleeping which has a serious effect on our health. Those who have prolonged sleeping problems are facing a serious medical condition and should see a qualified doctor when possible for help. Here is simple guide that can help you sleep better at night.

Try to create a natural pattern of waking up and sleeping around the same time every day. This means avoiding going to bed too early and oversleeping past your usual wake up time. Going to bed and getting up at radically different times everyday confuses your body clock. Try to establish a natural rhythm as much as you can.

Exercises and a bit of physical activity can help you sleep better at night. If you are having problem sleeping, try to be as active as you can during the day. If you are tired from physical activity, falling asleep is a natural and easy process for your body. If you remain inactive during the day, you will find it harder to sleep properly at night. Try walking, jogging, swimming or simple stretches close to your bed time.

Afternoon naps are great to refresh you during the day, but they may also keep you awake at night. If you feel sleepy during the day, get up, take a walk and get busy to keep from sleeping. Stretching is a good way to increase blood flow to the brain and keep you alert so that you don't sleep during the day. This will help you sleep better night.

> A warm bath or a glass of milk in the evening can help your body relax and prepare for sleep. A cold bath will wake you up and keep you up for several hours. Also avoid eating too late before bed.

12. How would you describe this sentence?

    a. A recommendation

    b. An opinion

    c. A fact

    d. A diagnosis

13. Which of the following is an alternative title for this article?

    a. Exercise and a good night's sleep

    b. Benefits of a good night's sleep

    c. Tips for a good night's sleep

    d. Lack of sleep is a serious medical condition

14. Which of the following cannot be inferred from this article?

   a. Biking is helpful for getting a good night's sleep

   b. Mental activity is helpful for getting a good night's sleep

   c. Eating bedtime snacks is not recommended

   d. Getting up at the same time is helpful for a good night's sleep

15. What is a disadvantage of taking naps?

   a. They may keep you awake.

   b. There are no disadvantages

   c. They may help you sleep better

   d. They may affect your diet

Question 16 refers to the following Table of Contents.

Contents

   Science Self-assessment 81
   Answer Key 91
   Science Tutorials 96
   Scientific Method 96
   Biology 99
   Heredity: Genes and Mutation 104
   Classification 108
   Ecology 110
   Chemistry 112
   Energy: Kinetic and Mechanical 126
   Energy: Work and Power 130
   Force: Newton's Three Laws 132

16. Consider the table of contents above. What page would you find information about natural selection and adaptation?

    a. 81
    b. 90
    c. 110
    d. 132

Questions 17 – 20 refer to the following passage.

Passage 5 - Pearl Harbor

A Day That Will Live in Infamy! Attack on Pearl Harbor
In 1941, the world was at war. The United States was trying to stay out of the conflict. In Europe, the countries of Germany and Italy had formed an alliance to expand their land and territory. Germany had already taken over Poland, Denmark, and parts of France. They were heading next toward England and due to all the fighting in Europe, there were battles taking place as far south as North Africa, where the German and Italian armies were fighting the British.

This got even worse when the Asian nation of Japan formed an alliance with Germany and Italy. Together, the three countries called themselves, the AXIS. Now, the war was in the Pacific as well as in Europe and Northern Africa. Many Americans felt that perhaps now was the time for the United States to join with its ally, Great Britain and stop the Axis from taking over more regions of the world.

In 1941, Franklin Roosevelt was President of the United States. His fear at the time was that Japan would try to take over many countries in Asia. He did not want to see that happen, so he moved some of the United States warships that had been stationed in San Diego, to the military base at Pearl Harbor, in Honolulu, Hawaii.

Japan quietly plotted their attack. They waited until the early hours of the morning on Sunday, December 7, 1941. Then,

350 Japanese war plans began to drop bombs on the U.S. ships at Pearl Harbor. The first bombs fell at 7:48 am and a mere 90 minutes later, the attack was over. Pearl Harbor was decimated. 8 battleships were damaged. Eleven ships were sunk and 300 U.S. planes were destroyed. Most devastating was the loss of life 2,400 U.S. military members was killed in the attack and 1,282 were injured.

President Roosevelt addressed the country via the radio and said "Today is a day that will live in infamy." He asked Congress to declare war on Japan. War was declared on Japan on December 8th and on Germany and Italy on December 11th. The United States had entered World War Two.

17. After reading the passage, what can we infer infamy means?

    a. Famous

    b. Remembered in a good way

    c. Remembered in a bad way

    d. Easily forgotten

18. What three countries formed the Axis?

    a. Italy, England, Germany

    b. United States, England, Italy

    c. Germany, Japan, Italy

    d. Germany, Japan, United States

19. What do you think was President Roosevelt's reason for moving warships to Pearl Harbor?

    a. He feared Japan would bomb San Diego

    b. He knew Japan was going to attack Pearl Harbor

    c. He was planning to attack Japan

    d. He wanted to try to protect Asian countries from Japanese takeover

20. Why do you think Japan chose a Sunday morning at 7:48 am for their attack?

    a. They knew the military slept late

    b. There is a law against bombing countries on a Sunday

    c. They wanted the attack to catch people by surprise

    d. That was the only free time they had to attack.

Questions 21 - 24 refer to the following recipe.

If You Have Allergies, You're Not Alone

People who experience allergies might joke that their immune systems have let them down or are seriously lacking. Truthfully though, people who experience allergic reactions or allergy symptoms during certain times of the year have heightened immune systems that are, "better" than those of people who have perfectly healthy but less militant immune systems.

Still, when a person has an allergic reaction, they are having an adverse reaction to a substance that is considered normal to most people. Mild allergic reactions usually have symptoms like itching, runny nose, red eyes, or bumps or discoloration of the skin. More serious allergic reactions, such as those to animal and insect poisons or certain foods, may result in the closing of the throat, swelling of the eyes, low blood pressure, inability to breath, and can even be fatal.

Different treatments help different allergies, and which one a person uses depends on the nature and severity of the allergy. It is recommended to patients with severe allergies to take extra precautions, such as carrying an EpiPen, which treats anaphylactic shock and may prevent death, always in order for the remedy to be readily available and more effective. When an allergy is not so severe, treatments may be used just relieve a person of uncomfortable symptoms. Over the counter allergy medicines treat milder symptoms, and can be bought at any grocery store and used in moderation to help people with allergies live normally.

There are many tests available to assess whether a person has allergies or what they may be allergic to, and advances in these tests and the medicine used to treat patients continues to improve. Despite this fact, allergies still affect many people throughout the year or even every day. Medicines used to treat allergies have side-effects, and it is difficult to bring the body into balance with the use of medicine. Regardless, many of those who live with allergies are grateful for what is available and find it useful in maintaining their lifestyles.

21. According to this passage, which group does the word "militant" belong in

    a. sickly, ailing, faint

    b. strength, power, vigor

    c. active, fighting, warring

    d. worn, tired, breaking down

22. The author says that "medicines used to treat allergies have side-effects of their own" to

    a. point out that doctors aren't very good at diagnosing and treating allergies

    b. argue that because of the large number of people with allergies, a cure will never be found

    c. explain that allergy medicines aren't cures and some compromise must be made

    d. argue that more wholesome remedies should be researched and medicines banned

23. It can be inferred that _____ recommend that some people with allergies carry medicine with them.

    a. the author

    b. doctors

    c. the makers of EpiPen

    d. people with allergies

24. The author has written this passage to

a. inform readers on symptoms of allergies so people with allergies can get help

b. persuade readers to be proud of having allergies

c. inform readers on different remedies so people with allergies receive the right help

d. describe different types of allergies, their symptoms, and their remedies

Questions 25 – 26 refer to the following email.

SUBJECT: MEDICAL STAFF CHANGES

To all staff:

This email is to advise you of a paper on recommended medical staff changes has been posted to the Human Resources website.

The contents are of primary interest to medical staff, other staff may be interested in reading it, particularly those in medical support roles.

The paper deals with several major issues:

1. Improving our ability to attract top quality staff to the hospital, and retain our existing staff. These changes will make our position and departmental names internationally recognizable and comparable with North American and North Asian departments and positions.

2. Improving our ability to attract top quality staff by introducing greater flexibility in the departmental structure.

3. General comments on issues to be further discussed relative to research staff.

The changes outlined in this paper are significant. I encourage you to read the document and send to me any comments you may have, so that it can be enhanced and improved.

Gordon Simms
Administrator,
Seven Oaks Regional Hospital

25. Are all hospital staff required to read the document posted to the Human Resources website?

    a. Yes all staff are required to read the document.

    b. No, reading the document is optional.

    c. Only medical staff are required to read the document.

    d. none of the above are correct.

26. Have the changes to medical staff been made?

    a. Yes, the changes have been made.

    b. No, the changes are only being discussed.

    c. Some of the changes have been made.

    d. None of the choices are correct.

Questions 27 – 30 refer to the following passage.

When a Poet Longs to Mourn, He Writes an Elegy

Poems are an expressive, especially emotional, form of writing. They have been in literature virtually from the time civilizations invented the written word. Poets often portrayed as moody, secluded, and even troubled, but this is because poets are introspective and feel deeply about the current events and cultural norms they are surrounded with. Poets often produce the most telling literature, giving insight into the society and mind-set they come from. This can be done in many forms.
The oldest types of poems often include many stanzas, may

or may not rhyme, and are more about telling a story than experimenting with language or words. The most common types of ancient poetry are epics, which are usually extremely long stories that follow a hero through his journey, or ellegies, which are often solemn in tone and used to mourn or lament something or someone. The Mesopotamians are often said to have invented the written word, and their literature is among the oldest in the world, including the epic poem titled "Epic of Gilgamesh." Similar in style and length to "Gilgamesh" is "Beowulf," an ellegy written in Old English and set in Scandinavia. These poems are often used by professors as the earliest examples of literature.

The importance of poetry was revived in the Renaissance. At this time, Europeans discovered the style and beauty of ancient Greek arts, and poetry was among those. Shakespeare is the most well-known poet of the time, and he used poetry not only to write poems but also to write plays for the theater. The most popular forms of poetry during the Renaissance included villanelles, (a nineteen-line poetic form) sonnets, as well as the epic. Poets during this time focused on style and form, and developed very specific rules and outlines for how an exceptional poem should be written.

As often happens in the arts, modern poets have rejected the constricting rules of Renaissance poets, and free form poems are much more popular. Some modern poems would read just like stories if they weren't arranged into lines and stanzas. It is difficult to tell which poems and poets will be the most important, because works of art often become more famous in hindsight, after the poet has died and society can look at itself without being in the moment. Modern poetry continues to develop, and will no doubt continue to change as values, thought, and writing continue to change.

Poems can be among the most enlightening and uplifting texts for a person to read if they are looking to connect with the past, connect with other people, or try to gain an understanding of what is happening in their time.

27. In summary, the author has written this passage

   a. as a foreword that will introduce a poem in a book or magazine

   b. because she loves poetry and wants more people to like it

   c. to give a brief history of poems

   d. to convince students to write poems

28. The author organizes the paragraphs mainly by

   a. moving chronologically, explaining which types of poetry were common in that time

   b. talking about new types of poems each paragraph and explaining them a little

   c. focusing on one poet or group of people and the poems they wrote

   d. explaining older types of poetry so she can talk about modern poetry

29. The author's claim that poetry has been around "virtually from the time civilizations invented the written word" is supported by the detail that

   a. Beowulf is written in Old English, which is not really in use any longer

   b. epic poems told stories about heroes

   c. the Renaissance poets tried to copy Greek poets

   d. the Mesopotamians are credited with both inventing the word and writing "Epic of Gilgamesh"

30. According to the passage, the word "telling" means

   a. speaking

   b. significant

   c. soothing

   d. wordy

MATHEMATICS

1. Divide 243 by 3^3

    a. 243
    b. 11
    c. 9
    d. 27

2. Solve the following equation $4(y + 6) = 3y + 30$

    a. $y = 20$
    b. $y = 6$
    c. $y = 30/7$
    d. $y = 30$

3. Divide $x^2 - y^2$ by $x - y$.

    a. $x - y$
    b. $x + y$
    c. xy
    d. $y - x$

4. Solve for x if, $10^2 \times 100^2 = 1000^x$

    a. $x = 2$
    b. $x = 3$
    c. $x = -2$
    d. $x = 0$

5. Given polynomials A = -2x⁴ + x² - 3x, B = x⁴ - x³ + 5 and C = x⁴ + 2x³ + 4x + 5, find A + B - C.

   a. $x^3 + x^2 + x + 10$
   b. $-3x^3 + x^2 - 7x + 10$
   c. $-2x^4 - 3x^3 + x^2 - 7x$
   d. $-3x^4 + x^3 + 2 - 7x$

6. Solve the inequality: $(x - 6)^2 \geq x^2 + 12$

   a. $(2, +\infty)$
   b. $(2, +\infty)$
   c. $(-\infty, 2]$
   d. $(12, +\infty)$

7. $7^5 - 3^5 =$

   a. 15,000
   b. 16,564
   c. 15,800
   d. 15,007

8. Divide $x^3 - 3x^2 + 3x - 1$ by $x - 1$.

   a. $x^2 - 1$
   b. $x^2 + 1$
   c. $x^2 - 2x + 1$
   d. $x^2 + 2x + 1$

9. Express 9 x 9 x 9 in exponential form and standard form.

   a. $9^3 = 719$
   b. $9^3 = 629$
   c. $9^3 = 729$
   d. $10^3 = 729$

Practice Test Questions 1

10. Using the factoring method, solve the quadratic equation: $x^2 - 5x - 6 = 0$

   a. -6 and 1
   b. -1 and 6
   c. 1 and 6
   d. -6 and -1

11. Divide 0.524 by 10^3

   a. 0.0524
   b. 0.000524
   c. 0.00524
   d. 524

12. Factor the polynomial $x^3y^3 - x^2y^8$.

   a. $x^2y^3(x - y^5)$
   b. $x^3y^3(1 - y^5)$
   c. $x^2y^2(x - y^6)$
   d. $xy^3(x - y^5)$

13. Find the solution for the following linear equation:
$5x/2 = 3x + 24/6$

   a. -1
   b. 0
   c. 1
   d. 2

14. $3^2 \times 3^5$

   a. 3^{17}
   b. 3^5
   c. 4^8
   d. 3^7

15. Solve the system, if a is some real number:

$ax + y = 1$
$x + ay = 1$

    a. $(1, a)$
    b. $(1/a + 1, 1)$
    c. $(1/(a + 1), 1/(a + 1))$
    d. $(a, 1/a + 1)$

16. Solve $3^5 \div 3^8$

    a. 3^3
    b. 3^5
    c. 3^6
    d. 3^4

17. Solve the linear equation: $3(x + 2) - 2(1 - x) = 4x + 5$

    a. -1
    b. 0
    c. 1
    d. 2

18. Simplify the following expression: $3x^a + 6a^x - x^a + (-5a^x) - 2x^a$

    a. $a^x + x^a$
    b. $a^x - x^a$
    c. a^x
    d. x^a

Practice Test Questions 1

19. Add polynomials $-3x^2 + 2x + 6$ and $-x^2 - x - 1$.

   a. $-2x^2 + x + 5$
   b. $-4x^2 + x + 5$
   c. $-2x^2 + 3x + 5$
   d. $-4x^2 + 3x + 5$

20. 10^4 is not equal to which of the following?

   a. 100,000
   b. 10 x 10 x 10 x 10
   c. 10^2 x 10^2
   d. 10,000

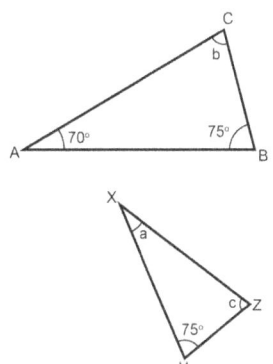

21. What are the respective values of a, b & c if both triangles are similar?

   a. 70°, 70°, 35°
   b. 70°, 35°, 70°
   c. 35°, 35°, 35°
   d. 70°, 35°, 35°

22. Consider 2 triangles, ABC and A'B'C', where:

BC = B' C'
AC = A' C'
RA = RA'

Are these 2 triangles congruent?

a. Yes
b. No
c. Not enough information

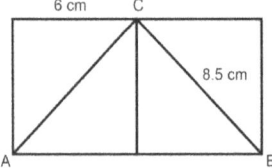

Note: figure not drawn to scale

23. Assuming the 2 quadrangles in the figure above are identical rectangles, what is the perimeter of △ABC in the above shape?

a. 25.5 cm
b. 27 cm
c. 30 cm
d. 29 cm

24. If angle α is equal to the expression 3π/2 - π/6 - π - π/3, find sinα.

a. 0
b. 1/2
c. 1
d. 3/2

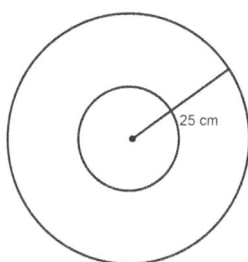

Note: figure not drawn to scale

25. What is the distance traveled by the wheel above, when it makes 175 revolutions?

    a. 87.5 π m
    b. 875 π m
    c. 8.75 π m
    d. 8750 π m

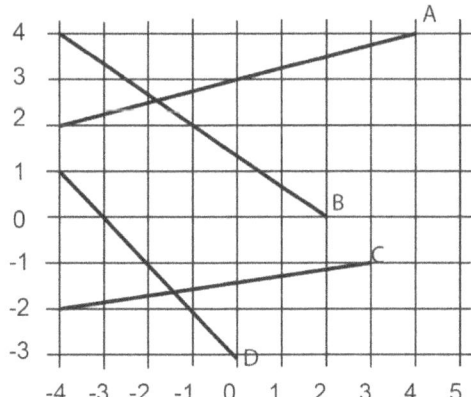

26. Which of the lines above represents the equation 2y − x = 4?

    a. A
    b. B
    c. C
    d. D

27. Find the sides of a right triangle whose sides are consecutive numbers.

    a. 1, 2, 3
    b. 2, 3, 4
    c. 3, 4, 5
    d. 4, 5, 6

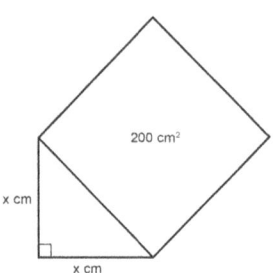

Note: figure not drawn to scale

28. Assuming the quadrangle in the figure above is a square, what is the length of the sides in the triangle above?

    a. 10
    b. 20
    c. 100
    d. 40

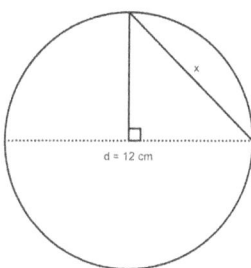

Note: figure not drawn to scale

29. Calculate the length of side x.

a. 6.46
b. 8.46
c. 3.6
d. 6.4

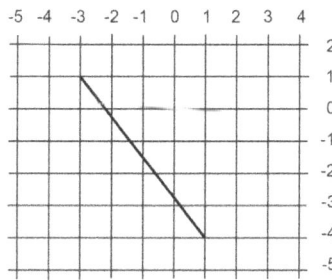

30. What is the slope of the line shown above?

a. 5/4
b. -4/5
c. -5/4
d. -4/5

WRITING

Directions: For questions 1 - 3, read the short passage answer the question.

Alvin Lee began playing guitar at an early age, and was influenced by his parents' passion for music and inspired by the likes of Chuck Berry and Scotty Moore. [1] Lee started his career as the lead vocalist and guitarist in a band named the Jaybirds at the famous Marquee Club in London in 1962. [2] A few years later the band changed its name to Ten Years After, and released its debut album under the new name. [3] Lee's lightning fast guitar playing at the Woodstock Festival gained him instant stardom and Lee was asked to tour the US. [4]

1. Which sentence in the second paragraph is the least relevant to the main idea of the second paragraph?

    a. 1
    b. 2
    c. 3
    d. 4

Curiosity was launched in late November 2011 from Cape Canaveral Air Force Station in Florida. [1] It successfully landed on Mars on August 6, 2012 searching for evidence of life. [2] The car sized robot, weighing about a ton, is equipped with all the technical capacities to carry out its mission to explore our neighbor for biological, geological and geochemical traces of life. [3] It will also test the Martian soil and surface to collect data about its planetary evolution and surface radiation. [4]

Practice Test Questions 1   193

2. Which sentence is the least relevant to the main idea of the third paragraph?

    a. 1
    b. 2
    c. 3
    d. 4

With an estimated 100,000 species, trees represent 25 percent of all living plant species. Most tree species grow in tropical regions of the world and many of these areas have not been surveyed by botanists, making species diversity poorly understood. The earliest trees were tree ferns and horsetails, which grew in forests in the Carboniferous period. Tree ferns still survive, but the only surviving horsetails are no longer in tree form. Later, in the Triassic period, conifers and ginkgos, appeared, followed by flowering plants after that in the Cretaceous period. [5]

3. Choose the correct list below, ranked from oldest to youngest trees.

    a. Flowering plants, conifers and ginkgos, tree ferns and horsetails

    b. Tree ferns and horsetails, conifers and ginkgos, flowering plants

    c. Tree ferns and horsetails, flowering plants, conifers and ginkgos

    d. Conifers and ginkgos, tree ferns and horsetails, flowering plants

Directions: Choose the word or phrase that best completes the sentence.

4. The Ford Motor Company was named for Henry Ford, _____ had founded the company.

    a. which

    b. who

    c. whose

    d. None of the options are correct.

5. Thomas Edison _____ as the greatest inventor since he invented the light bulb, television, motion pictures, and phonograph.

    a. has always been known

    b. was always been known

    c. must have had been always known

    d. None of the options are correct.

6. The weatherman on Channel 6 said that this has been the _____ summer on record.

    a. most hottest

    b. hottest

    c. hotter

    d. None of the options are correct.

7. Although Joe is tall for his age, his brother Elliot is _____ of the two.

    a. tallest

    b. tall of the two.

    c. the taller

    d. None of the options are correct.

Practice Test Questions 1

8. When KISS came to town, all the tickets ____ sold out before I could buy one.

    a. will be

    b. had been

    c. were being

    d. None of the options are correct.

9. The rules of most sports ____ more complicated than we often realize.

    a. are

    b. is

    c. was

    d. None of the options are correct.

10. Neither of the Wright Brothers ____ any doubts that they would be successful with their flying machine.

    a. have

    b. has

    c. had

    d. None of the options are correct.

11. The Titanic ____ mere days into its maiden voyage.

    a. will already sunk

    b. sank

    c. had sank

    d. None of the choices are correct.

12. When he's _____ friends, Robert seems confident.

   a. None of the choices are correct.

   b. between

   c. among

13. His home was _____ than we expected.

   a. The sentence is correct.

   b. farther

   c. None of the choices are correct.

14. The tables were _____ by the students.

   a. laid

   b. lay

   c. lie

   d. None of the choices are correct.

15. Each boy and girl _____ given a toy.

   a. were

   b. was

   c. Either A or B can be used.

   d. None of the choices are correct.

16. His measles _____ getting better.

   a. is

   b. are

   c. Either A or B can be used.

   d. None of the choices are correct.

Practice Test Questions 1

17. Despite the bad weather yesterday, he ___ still attend the party.

    a. The sentence is correct.

    b. could

    c. may

    d. None of the choices are correct.

18. Choose the sentence with the correct punctuation.

    a. To make chicken soup you must first buy a chicken.

    b. To make chicken soup you must first, buy a chicken.

    c. To make chicken soup, you must first buy a chicken.

    d. None of the choices are correct.

19. Choose the sentence with the correct punctuation.

    a. To travel around the globe, you have to drive 25000 miles.

    b. To travel around the globe, you have to drive, 25000 miles.

    c. None of the choices are correct.

    d. To travel around the globe, you have to drive 25,000 miles.

20. Choose the sentence with the correct punctuation.

    a. The dog loved chasing bones, but never ate them; it was running that he enjoyed.

    b. The dog loved chasing bones; but never ate them, it was running that he enjoyed.

    c. The dog loved chasing bones, but never ate them, it was running that he enjoyed.

    d. None of the choices are correct.

21. Choose the sentence with the correct punctuation.

a. However, I believe that he didn't really try that hard.
b. However I believe that he didn't really try that hard.
c. None of the choices are correct.
d. However: I believe that he didn't really try that hard.

22. Choose the sentence that is written correctly.

a. Any girl that fails the test loses their admission.
b. Any girl that fails the test loses our admission.
c. Any girl that fails the test loses <u>her</u> admission.
d. None of the choices are correct.

23. Choose the sentence that is written correctly.

a. He ought to be back by now.
b. He ought be back by now.
c. He ought come back by now.
d. None of the choices are correct.

24. Choose the sentence that is written correctly.

a. The man as well as his son has arrived
b. The man as well as his son have arrived.
c. None of the choices are correct.

25. Choose the sentence that is written correctly.

a. Mark and Peter have talked to each other.
b. Mark and Peter have talked to one another.
c. None of the choices are correct.

26. Choose the sentence that is written correctly.

a. Christians believe that their lord have raised.
b. Christians believe that their lord has risen.
c. Christians believe that their lord have raise.
d. None of the choices are correct.

27. Choose the sentence that is written correctly.

a. Here are the names of people whom you should contact.
b. Here are the names of people who you should contact
c. None of the choices are correct.

28. Choose the sentence that is written correctly.

a. The World Health Organization (WHO) are meeting by January.
b. The World Health Organization (WHO) is meeting by January.
c. None of the choices are correct.

29. Choose the sentence that is written correctly.

a. They will have to retire when they reach 60 years of age.
b. They shall have to retire when they reach 60 years of age.
c. None of the choices are correct.

Directions: Choose the sentence that best support the topic sentence below.

30. Volcanoes occur because the planet's crust is broken into 17 major tectonic plates that float on a hotter, softer layer in the Earth's mantle.

    a. Therefore, volcanoes are generally found where tectonic plates are diverging or converging.

    b. Volcanoes generally cause extensive damage to property.

    c. Volcanoes do not often erupt, but can be spectacular when they do.

    c. Most volcanoes are far from major urban centers.

Answer Key

Section 1 – Reading

1. A
The correct answer because that fact is stated directly in the passage. The passage explains that Anne taught Helen to hear by allowing her to feel the vibrations in her throat.

2. B
We can infer that Anne is a patient teacher because she did not leave or lose her temper when Helen bit or hit her; she just kept trying to teach Helen. Choice B is incorrect because Anne taught Helen to read and talk. Choice C is incorrect because Anne could hear. She was partially blind, not deaf. Choice D is incorrect because it does not have to do with patience.

3. A
The passage states that it was hard for anyone but Anne to understand Helen when she spoke. Choice A is incorrect because the passage does not mention Helen spoke a foreign language. Choice C is incorrect because there is no mention of how quiet or loud Helen's voice was. Choice D is incorrect because we know from reading the passage that Helen did learn to speak.

4. B
This question tests the reader's summarization skills. The other choices A, B, and C focus on portions of the second paragraph that are too narrow and do not relate to the specific portion of text in question. The complexity of the sentence may mislead students into selecting one of these answers, but rearranging or restating the sentence will lead the reader to the correct answer. In addition, choice A makes an assumption that may or may not be true about the intentions of the company, choice B focuses on one product rather than the idea of the products, and choice C makes an assumption about women that may or may not be true and is not supported by the text.

5. D
This question tests the reader's summarization skills. The question is asking very generally about the message of the passage, and the title, "Ways Characters Communicate in Theater," is one indication of that. The other choices A, B, and C are all directly from the text, and therefore readers may be inclined to select one of them, but are too specific to encapsulate the entirety of the passage and its message.

6. B
The paragraph on soliloquies mentions "To be or not to be," and it is from the context of that paragraph that readers may understand that because "To be or not to be" is a soliloquy, Hamlet will be introspective, or thoughtful, while delivering it. It is true that actors deliver soliloquies alone, and may be "solitary" (choice A), but "thoughtful" (choice B) is more true to the overall idea of the paragraph. Readers may choose C because drama and theater can be used interchangeably and the passage mentions that soliloquies are unique to theater (and therefore drama), but this answer is not specific enough to the paragraph in question. Readers may pick up on the theme of life and death and Hamlet's true intentions and select that he is "hopeless" (choice D), but those themes are not discussed either by this paragraph or passage, as a close textual reading and analysis confirms.

7. C
This question tests the reader's grammatical skills. Choice B seems logical, but parenthesis are actually considered to be a stronger break in a sentence than commas are, and along this line of thinking, actually disrupt the sentence more.

Choices A and D make comparisons between theater and film that are simply not made in the passage, and may or may not be true. This detail does clarify the statement that asides are most unique to theater by adding that it is not completely unique to theater, which may have been why the author didn't chose not to delete it and instead used parentheses to designate the detail's importance (choice C).

8. A
Low blood sugar occurs both in diabetics and healthy adults.

Practice Test Questions 1

9. B
None of the statements are the author's opinion.

10. A
The author's purpose is the inform.

11. A
The only statement that is not a detail is, "A doctor can diagnosis this medical condition by asking the patient questions and testing."

12. A
This sentence is a recommendation.

13. C
Tips for a good night's sleep is the best alternative title for this article.

14. B
Mental activity is helpful for a good night's sleep is cannot be inferred from this article.

15. A
From the passage, one disadvantage of taking naps is they may keep you awake at night.

16. A
Based on the partial table of contents, this book is most likely about how to answer multiple choice.

17. C
To be infamous means to be remembered for an evil or terrible action. Therefore, the word infamy means to remember a bad or terrible thing. Choice A is incorrect because being famous is not the same as being infamous. Choice B is incorrect because the attack on Pearl Harbor was not good. Choice D is incorrect because Pearl Harbor was not forgotten.

18. C
Each answer choice except choice C contains the name of at least one country that was not part of the AXIS powers.

19. D
It is stated in the passage. Choice A is not correct because there was no indication that Japan would attack San Diego. Choice B is incorrect because the attack on Pearl Harbor was a surprise. Choice C is incorrect because Roosevelt was not planning to attack Japan.

20. C
The passage clearly states that Japan planned a surprise attack. They chose that early time to catch the U.S. military off guard. Choice A is incorrect because the military does not sleep late. Choice B is incorrect because there is no law against bombing countries. Choice D is incorrect because it makes no sense.

21. C
This question tests the reader's vocabulary skills. The uses of the negatives "but" and "less," especially right next to each other, may confuse readers into answering with choices A or D, which list words that are antonyms to "militant." Readers may also be confused by the comparison of healthy people with what is being described as an overly healthy person--both people are good, but the reader may look for which one is "worse" in the comparison, and therefore stray toward the antonym words. One key to understanding the meaning of "militant" if the reader is unfamiliar with it is to look at the root of the word; readers can then easily associate it with "military" and gain a sense of what the word signifies: defense (especially considered that the immune system defends the body). Choice C is correct over choice B because "militant" is an adjective, just as the words in choice C are, whereas the words in choice B are nouns.

22. C
This question tests the reader's understanding of function within writing. The other choices are details included surrounding the quoted text, and may therefore confuse the reader. A somewhat contradicts what is said earlier in the paragraph, which is that tests and treatments are improving, and probably doctors are along with them, but the paragraph doesn't actually mention doctors, and the subject of the question is the medicine. Choice B may seem correct to readers who aren't careful to understand that, while the

author does mention the large number of people affected, the author is touching on the realities of living with allergies, rather than the likelihood of curing all allergies. Similarly, while the author does mention the "balance" of the body, which is easily associated with "wholesome," the author is not really making an argument and especially is not making an extreme statement that allergy medicines should be outlawed. Again, because the article's tone is on living with allergies, choice C is an appropriate choice that fits with the title and content of the text.

23. B
This question tests the reader's inference skills. The text does not state who is doing the recommending, but the use of the "patients," as well as the general context of the passage, lends itself to the logical partner, "doctors," choice B. The author does mention the recommendation but doesn't present it as her own (i.e. "I recommend that"), so choice A may be eliminated. It may seem plausible that people with allergies (choice D) may recommend medicines or products to other people with allergies, but the text does not necessarily support this interaction taking place. Choice C may be selected because the EpiPen is specifically mentioned, but the use of the phrase "such as" when it is introduced is not limiting enough to assume the recommendation is coming from its creators.

24. D
This question tests the reader's global understanding of the text. Choice D includes the main topics of the three body paragraphs, and isn't too focused on a specific aspect or quote from the text, as the other questions are, giving a skewed summary of what the author intended. The reader may be drawn to choice B because of the title of the passage and the use of words like "better," but the message of the passage is larger and more general than this.

25. B
Reading the document posted to the Human Resources website is optional.

26. B
The document is recommended changes and have not be implemented yet.

27. C
This question tests the reader's summarization skills. The use of the word "actually" in describing what kind of people poets are, as well as other moments like this, may lead readers to selecting choices B or D, but the author is more information than trying to persuade readers. The author gives no indication that she loves poetry (choice B) or that people, students specifically (D), should write poems. Choice A is incorrect because the style and content of this paragraph do not match those of a foreword; forewords usually focus on the history or ideas of a specific poem to introduce it more fully and help it stand out against other poems. The author here focuses on several poems and gives broad statements. Instead, she tells a kind of story about poems, giving three very broad time periods in which to discuss them, thereby giving a brief history of poetry, as choice C states.

28. A
This question tests the reader's summarization skills. Key words in the topic sentences of each of the paragraphs ("oldest," "Renaissance," "modern") should give the reader an idea that the author is moving chronologically. The opening and closing sentence-paragraphs are broad and talk generally. B seems reasonable, but epic poems are mentioned in two paragraphs, eliminating the idea that only new types of poems are used in each paragraph. Choice C is also easily eliminated because the author clearly mentions several different poets, groups of people, and poems. Choice D also seems reasonable, considering that the author does move from older forms of poetry to newer forms, but use of "so (that)" makes this statement false, for the author gives no indication that she is rushing (the paragraphs are about the same size) or that she prefers modern poetry.

29. D
This question tests the reader's attention to detail. The key word is "invented"--it ties together the Mesopotamians, who invented the written word, and the fact that they, as the inventors, also invented and used poetry. The other selections focus on other details mentioned in the passage, such as that the Renaissance's admiration of the Greeks (choice C) and that Beowulf is in Old English (choice A). Choice B may seem like an attractive answer because it is unlike the oth-

ers and because the idea of heroes seems rooted in ancient and early civilizations.

30. B
This question tests the reader's vocabulary and contextualization skills. "Telling" is not an unusual word, but it may be used here in a way that is not familiar to readers, as an adjective rather than a verb in gerund form. A may seem like the obvious answer to a reader looking for a verb to match the use they are familiar with. If the reader understands that the word is being used as an adjective and that choice A is a ploy, they may opt to select choice D, "wordy," but it does not make sense in context. Choice C can be easily eliminated, and doesn't have any connection to the paragraph or passage. "Significant" (choice B) makes sense contextually, especially relative to the phrase "give insight" used later in the sentence.

MATHEMATICS

1. C
243/3 x 3 x 3 = 243/27 = 9

2. B
4y + 24 = 3y + 30, = 4y − 3y + 24 = 30, = y + 24 = 30, = y = 30 − 24, = y = 6

3. B
$(x^2 - y^2) / (x - y) = x + y$

$\frac{-(x^2 - xy)}{xy - y^2}$

$\frac{-(xy - y^2)}{0}$

4. A
10 x 10 x 100 x 100 = 1000^x, =100 x 10,000 = 1000^x, = 1,000,000 = 1000^x = x = 2

5. C
We are asked to find A + B − C. By paying attention to the

sign distribution; we write the polynomials and operate:

$A + B - C = (-2x^4 + x^2 - 3x) + (x^4 - x^3 + 5) - (x^4 + 2x^3 + 4x + 5)$

$= -2x^4 + x^2 - 3x + x^4 - x^3 + 5 - x^4 - 2x^3 - 4x - 5$

$= -2x^4 + x^4 - x^4 - x^3 - 2x^3 + x^2 - 3x - 4x + 5 - 5$ ... similar terms written together to ease summing/substituting.

$= -2x^4 - 3x^3 + x^2 - 7x$

6. C
To find the solution for the inequality, we need to simplify it first:

$(x - 6)^2 \geq x^2 + 12$ ... we can write the open form of the left side:

$x^2 - 12x + 36 \geq x^2 + 12$ ... x^2 terms on both sides cancel:

$-12x + 36 \geq 12$ ... Now, we aim to have x alone on one side. So, we subtract 36 from both sides:

$-12x + 36 - 36 \geq 12 - 36$

$-12x \geq -24$ ... We divide both sides by -12. This means that the inequality will change its direction:

$x \leq 2$ ... x can be 2 or a smaller value.

This result is shown by $(-\infty, 2]$.

7. B
(7 x 7 x 7 x 7 x 7) - (3 x 3 x 3 x 3 x 3) = 16,807 – 243 = 16,564.

8. C
$(x^3 - 3x^2 + 3x - 1) / (x - 1) = x^2 - 2x + 1$
$\underline{-(x^3 - x^2)}$
$\quad\quad -2x^2 + 3x - 1$
$\quad\underline{-(-2x^2 + 2x)}$
$\quad\quad\quad\quad x - 1$

$\underline{-(x - 1)}$
0

9. C
Exponential form is 9^3 and standard from is 729

10. B
$x^2 - 5x - 6 = 0$

We try to separate the middle term -5x to find common factors with x^2 and -6 separately:

$x^2 - 6x + x - 6 = 0$ ... Here, we see that x is a common factor for x^2 and -6x:

$x(x - 6) + x - 6 = 0$ ... Here, we have x times $x - 6$ and 1 time $x - 6$ summed up. This means that we have $x + 1$ times $x - 6$:

$(x + 1)(x - 6) = 0$ ... This is true when either or both expressions in the parenthesis are equal to zero:

$x + 1 = 0 ... x = -1$

$x - 6 = 0 ... x = 6$

-1 and 6 are the solutions for this quadratic equation.

11. B
$0.524 / (10 * 10 * 10) = 0.524/1000$ ... This means that we need to carry the decimal point 3 decimals left from the point it is now:

= 0.0.0.0.524 = 0.000524

12. A
We need to find the greatest common divisor of the two terms to factor the expression. We should remember that if the bases of exponent numbers are the same, the multiplication of two terms is found by summing the powers and writing on the same base. Similarly; when dividing, the power of the divisor is subtracted from the power of the divided.
Both x^3y^3 and x^2y^8 contain x^2 and y^3. So;

$x^3y^3 - x^2y^8 = x * x^2y^3 - y^5 * x^2y^3$ ... We can carry x^2y^3 out as the factor:

$= x^2y^3(x - y^5)$

13. D
Our aim is to collect the knowns on one side, and the unknowns (x terms) on the other side:

$5x/2 = (3x + 24)/6$ ... First, we can simplify the denominators of both sides by 2:

$5x = (3x + 24)/3$ ... Now, Cross multiply:

$15x = 3x + 24$

$15x - 3x = 24$

$12x = 24$

$x = 24/12 = 2$

14. D
When multiplying exponents with the same base, add the exponents. $3^2 \times 3^5 = 3^{2+5} = 3^7$

15. C
Solving the system means finding x and y. Since we also have a in the system, we will find x and y depending on a.

We can obtain y by using the equation $ax + y = 1$:

$y = 1 - ax$ ... Then, we can insert this value into the second equation:

$x + a(1 - ax) = 1$

$x + a - a^2x = 1$

$x - a^2x = 1 - a$

$x(1 - a^2) = 1 - a$ ... We need to obtain x alone:

$x = (1 - a)/(1 - a^2)$ ... Here, $1 - a^2 = (1 - a)(1 + a)$ is used:

$x = (1 - a)/((1 - a)(1 + a))$ ... Simplifying by $(1 - a)$:

$x = 1/(a + 1)$ ... Now we know the value of x. By using either of the equations, we can find the value of y. Let us use $y = 1 - ax$:

$y = 1 - a * 1/(a + 1)$

$y = 1 - a/(a + 1)$ ... By writing on the same denominator:

$y = ((a + 1) - a)/(a + 1)$

$y = (a + 1 - a)/(a + 1)$ ... a and -a cancel:

$y = 1/(a + 1)$ ... x and y are found to be equal.

The solution of the system is $(1/(a + 1), 1/(a + 1))$

16. A
To divide exponents with the same base, subtract the exponents. $3^{8-5} = 3^3$

17. C
To solve the linear equation, we operate the knowns and unknowns within each other and try to obtain x term (which is the unknown) alone on one side of the equation:

$3(x + 2) - 2(1 - x) = 4x + 5$ ... We remove the parenthesis by distributing the factors:

$3x + 6 - 2 + 2x = 4x + 5$

$5x + 4 = 4x + 5$

$5x - 4x = 5 - 4$

$x = 1$

18. C
$3x^a + 6a^x - x^a + (-5a^x) - 2x^a = 3x^a + 6a^x - x^a - 5a^x - 2x^a = a^x$

19. B
By paying attention to the sign distribution; we write the polynomials and operate:
$(-3x^2 + 2x + 6) + (-x^2 - x - 1)$

$= -3x^2 + 2x + 6 - x^2 - x - 1$

$= -3x^2 - x^2 + 2x - x + 6 - 1$ ... similar terms written together to ease summing/substituting.

$= -4x^2 + x + 5$

20. A
10^4 is not equal to 100,000
$10^4 = 10 \times 10 \times 10 \times 10 = 10^2 \times 10^2 = 10,000$

21. D

Comparing angles on similar triangles, a, b and c will be 70°, 35°, 35°

22. A

Yes the triangles are congruent.

23. D

Perimeter of triangle ABC is asked.
Perimeter of a triangle = sum of all three sides.

Here, Perimeter of $\triangle ABC$ = |AC| + |CB| + |AB|.

Since the triangle is located in the middle of two adjacent and identical rectangles, we find the side lengths using these rectangles:

|AB| = 6 + 6 = 12 cm

|CB| = 8.5 cm

|AC| = |CB| = 8.5 cm

Perimeter = |AC| + |CB| + |AB| = 8.5 + 8.5 + 12 = 29 cm

24. A

First, we need to simplify the value of angle α:

α = $3\pi/2 - \pi/6 - \pi - \pi/3$ ... by equating the denominators at 6:

α = $9\pi/6 - \pi/6 - 6\pi/6 - 2\pi/6$

α = $(9 - 1 - 6 - 2)\pi/6$

α = $0 * \pi /6$

α = 0

sinα = sin0° = 0

25. A

The wheel travels 2πr distance when it makes one revolution. Here, r stands for the radius. The radius is given as 25 cm in the figure. So,

$2\pi r = 2\pi * 25 = 50\pi$ cm is the distance traveled in one revolution.

In 175 revolutions: $175 * 50\pi = 8750\pi$ cm is traveled.

We are asked to find the distance in meter.

1 m = 100 cm So;

8750π cm = 8750π / 100 = 87.5π m

26. A
If a line represents an equation, all points on that line should satisfy the equation. Meaning that all (x, y) pairs present on the line should be able to verify that 2y - x is equal to 4. We can find out the correct line by trying a (x, y) point existing on each line. It is easier to choose points on the intersection of the gridlines:
Let us try the point (4, 4) on line A:

2 * 4 - 4 = 4

8 - 4 = 4

4 = 4 ... this is a correct result, so the equation for line A is 2y - x = 4.

Let us try other points to check the other lines:

Point (-1, 2) on line B:

2 * 2 - (-1) = 4

4 + 1 = 4

5 = 4 ... this is a wrong result, so the equation for line B is not 2y - x = 4.

Point (3, -1) on line C:

2 * (-1) - 3 = 4

-2 - 3 = 4

-5 = 4 ... this is a wrong result, so the equation for line C is not 2y - x = 4.

Point (-2, -1) on line D:

2 * (-1) - (-2) = 4

-2 + 2 = 4

0 = 4 ... this is a wrong result, so the equation for line D is not 2y - x = 4.

27. C
In a right angle, Pythagorean Theorem is applicable:
$a^2 + b^2 = c^2$ ... Here, a and b represent the adjacent and opposite sides, c represents the hypotenuse. Hypotenuse is larger than the other two sides.

In this question, we need to try each answer choice by applying $a^2 + b^2 = c^2$ to see if it is satisfied; by inserting the largest number into c:

a. 1, 2, 3:

$1^2 + 2^2 = 3^2$

1 + 4 = 9

5 = 9 ... This is not correct, so answer choice does not represent a right angle whose sides are consecutive numbers.

b. 2, 3, 4:

$2^2 + 3^2 = 4^2$

4 + 9 = 16

13 = 16 ... This is not correct, so this answer choice does not represent a right angle whose sides are consecutive numbers.

c. 3, 4, 5:

$3^2 + 4^2 = 5^2$

9 + 16 = 25

25 = 25 ... This is correct, 3, 4, 5 are also consecutive numbers; so this answer choice represents a right angle whose sides are consecutive numbers.

d. 4, 5, 6:

$4^2 + 5^2 = 6^2$

$16 + 25 = 36$

41 = 36 ... This is not correct, so this answer choice does not represent a right angle whose sides are consecutive numbers.

28. A
If we call one side of the square "a," the area of the square will be a^2.

We know that $a^2 = 200$ cm².

On the other hand; there is an isosceles right triangle.
Pythagorean Theorem:
(Hypotenuse)² = (Perpendicular)² + (Base)²
$h^2 = a^2 + b^2$

Given: $h^2 = 200$, a = b = x
Then, $x^2 + x^2 = 200$, $2x^2 = 200$, $x^2 = 100$
x = 10

29. B
In the question, we have a right triangle formed inside the circle. We are asked to find the length of the hypotenuse of this triangle. We can find the other two sides of the triangle by using circle properties:

The diameter of the circle is equal to 12 cm. The legs of the right triangle are the radii of the circle; so they are 6 cm long.

Pythagorean Theorem:
(Hypotenuse)² = (Perpendicular)² + (Base)²
$h^2 = a^2 + b^2$

Given: d (diameter)= 12 & r (radius) = a = b = 6
$h^2 = a^2 + b^2$
$h^2 = 6^2 + 6^2$, $h^2 = 36 + 36$

$h^2 = 72$
$h = 8.46$

30. C
Slope (m) = change in y / change in x

$(x_1, y_1) = (-3, 1)$ & $(x_2, y_2) = (1, -4)$
Slope = $[-4 - 1]/[1-(-3)] = -5/4$

WRITING

1. A
Sentence 1 is least relevant, "Alvin Lee began playing guitar at an early age, and was influenced by his parents' passion for music and inspired by the likes of Chuck Berry and Scotty Moore."

This sentence talks about Lee's motivation rather than his achievements, which is the main topic of the paragraph. Other sentences are related to a significant extent, but this sentence deviates from the main idea the most.

2. A
Sentence 1 is the least relevant. "Curiosity was launched in late November 2011 from Cape Canaveral Air Force Station in Florida."

This paragraph talks about the objectives of the rover. All sentences other than sentence 2 mention the objectives. This sentence, however, informs us when the spacecraft was launched.

3. B
Here is the passage with the oldest to youngest trees

The earliest trees were [1] tree ferns and horsetails, which grew in forests in the Carboniferous period. Tree ferns still survive, but the only surviving horsetails are no longer in tree form. Later, in the Triassic period, [2] conifers and ginkgos, appeared, [3] followed by flowering plants after that in the Cretaceous period

4. B
The sentence refers to a person, so "who" is the only correct choice.

5. A
The sentence requires the past perfect "has always been known." The clue to this tense is the use of "since."

6. B
The superlative, "hottest," is used when expressing a temperature greater than that of anything to which it is being compared.

7. C
When comparing two items, use "the taller." When comparing more than two items, use "the tallest."

8. B
The past perfect form is used to describe an event that occurred in the past and before another event.

9. A
The subject is "rules" so the present tense plural form, "are," is used to agree with "realize."

10. C
The simple past tense, "had," is correct because it refers to completed action in the past.

11. B
The simple past tense, "sank," is correct because it refers to completed action in the past.

12. C
Among vs. Between. 'Among' is for more than 2 items, and 'between' is only for 2 items.

When he's among friends (many or more than 2), Robert seems confident, but, between you and me (two), he is very shy.

13. B
Further vs. Farther. 'Farther' is used for physical distance, and 'further' is used for figurative distance.

14. A
The verb "lay" should always take an object. Here the subject is the table. The three forms of the verb lay are: lay, laid and laid. The sentence above is in past tense.

15. B
Use the singular verb form when nouns are qualified with "every" or "each," even if they are joined by 'and. '

16. B
Use a plural verb for nouns like measles, tongs, trousers, riches, scissors etc.

17. B
Use "could," the past tense of "can" to express ability or capacity.

18. C
Comma separate phrases.

19. D
The comma separates clauses and numbers are separated with a comma. The correct sentence is,
'To travel around the globe, you have to drive 25,000 miles.'

20. A
The dog loved chasing bones, but never ate them; it was running that he enjoyed.

21. A
When using 'however,' place a comma before and after, except when however begins the sentence.

22. C
Words such as neither, each, many, either, every, everyone, everybody and any should take a singular pronoun.

23. A
The verb "ought" can be used to express desirability, duty and probability. The verb is usually followed by "to."

24. A
When two subjects are linked with "with" or "as well," use the verb form that matches the first subject.

25. A
When you use 'each other' it should be used for two things or people. When you use 'one another' it should be used for things and people above two

26. B
The verb rise ('to go up', 'to ascend.') can appear in three forms, rise, rose, and risen. The verb should not take an object.

27. A
The sentence is correct. Use "whom" in the objective case, and use "who" a subjective case.

28. B
Use a singular verb with a proper noun in plural form that refers to a single entity. Here, the The World Health Organization is a single entity, although it is made up on many members.

29. A
Will is used in the second or third person (they, he, she and you), while shall is used in the first person (I and we). Both verbs are used to express futurity.

30. A
Sentence A continues directly the discussion about tectonic plates. The other choices diverge from this central idea.

PRACTICE TEST QUESTIONS SET 2

The questions below are not the same as you will find on the PERT - that would be too easy! And nobody knows what the questions will be and they change all the time. Below are general questions that cover the same subject areas as the PERT. So, while the format and exact wording of the questions may differ slightly, and change from year to year, if you can answer the questions below, you will have no problem with the PERT.

For the best results, take these practice test questions as if it were the real exam. Set aside time when you will not be disturbed, and a location that is quiet and free of distractions. Read the instructions carefully, read each question carefully, and answer to the best of your ability.
Use the bubble answer sheets provided. When you have completed the Practice Questions, check your answer against the Answer Key and read the explanation provided.

Do not attempt more than one set of practice test questions in one day. After completing the first practice test, wait two or three days before attempting the second set of questions.

Reading

	A B C D E		A B C D E
1	○ ○ ○ ○ ○	21	○ ○ ○ ○ ○
2	○ ○ ○ ○ ○	22	○ ○ ○ ○ ○
3	○ ○ ○ ○ ○	23	○ ○ ○ ○ ○
4	○ ○ ○ ○ ○	24	○ ○ ○ ○ ○
5	○ ○ ○ ○ ○	25	○ ○ ○ ○ ○
6	○ ○ ○ ○ ○	26	○ ○ ○ ○ ○
7	○ ○ ○ ○ ○	27	○ ○ ○ ○ ○
8	○ ○ ○ ○ ○	28	○ ○ ○ ○ ○
9	○ ○ ○ ○ ○	29	○ ○ ○ ○ ○
10	○ ○ ○ ○ ○	30	○ ○ ○ ○ ○
11	○ ○ ○ ○ ○		
12	○ ○ ○ ○ ○		
13	○ ○ ○ ○ ○		
14	○ ○ ○ ○ ○		
15	○ ○ ○ ○ ○		
16	○ ○ ○ ○ ○		
17	○ ○ ○ ○ ○		
18	○ ○ ○ ○ ○		
19	○ ○ ○ ○ ○		
20	○ ○ ○ ○ ○		

Mathematics

	A	B	C	D	E		A	B	C	D	E
1	○	○	○	○	○	21	○	○	○	○	○
2	○	○	○	○	○	22	○	○	○	○	○
3	○	○	○	○	○	23	○	○	○	○	○
4	○	○	○	○	○	24	○	○	○	○	○
5	○	○	○	○	○	25	○	○	○	○	○
6	○	○	○	○	○	26	○	○	○	○	○
7	○	○	○	○	○	27	○	○	○	○	○
8	○	○	○	○	○	28	○	○	○	○	○
9	○	○	○	○	○	29	○	○	○	○	○
10	○	○	○	○	○	30	○	○	○	○	○
11	○	○	○	○	○						
12	○	○	○	○	○						
13	○	○	○	○	○						
14	○	○	○	○	○						
15	○	○	○	○	○						
16	○	○	○	○	○						
17	○	○	○	○	○						
18	○	○	○	○	○						
19	○	○	○	○	○						
20	○	○	○	○	○						

Writing Skills

	A	B	C	D	E			A	B	C	D	E
1	○	○	○	○	○		21	○	○	○	○	○
2	○	○	○	○	○		22	○	○	○	○	○
3	○	○	○	○	○		23	○	○	○	○	○
4	○	○	○	○	○		24	○	○	○	○	○
5	○	○	○	○	○		25	○	○	○	○	○
6	○	○	○	○	○		26	○	○	○	○	○
7	○	○	○	○	○		27	○	○	○	○	○
8	○	○	○	○	○		28	○	○	○	○	○
9	○	○	○	○	○		29	○	○	○	○	○
10	○	○	○	○	○		30	○	○	○	○	○
11	○	○	○	○	○							
12	○	○	○	○	○							
13	○	○	○	○	○							
14	○	○	○	○	○							
15	○	○	○	○	○							
16	○	○	○	○	○							
17	○	○	○	○	○							
18	○	○	○	○	○							
19	○	○	○	○	○							
20	○	○	○	○	○							

Part 1 – Reading and Language Arts

Questions 1 - 4 refer to the following passage.

Passage 1 - The Crusades

In 1095 Pope Urban II proclaimed the First Crusade with the intent and stated goal to restore Christian access to holy places in and around Jerusalem. Over the next 200 years there were 6 major crusades and numerous minor crusades in the fight for control of the "Holy Land." Historians are divided on the real purpose of the Crusades, some believing that it was part of a purely defensive war against Islamic conquest; some see them as part of a long-running conflict at the frontiers of Europe; and others see them as confident, aggressive, papal-led expansion attempts by Western Christendom. The impact of the crusades was profound, and judgment of the Crusaders ranges from laudatory to highly critical. However, all agree that the Crusades and wars waged during those crusades were brutal and often bloody. Several hundred thousand Roman Catholic Christians joined the Crusades, they were Christians from all over Europe.

Europe at the time was under the Feudal System, so while the Crusaders made vows to the Church, they also were beholden to their Feudal Lords. This led to the Crusaders not only fighting the Saracen, the commonly used word for Muslim at the time, but also each other for power and economic gain in the Holy Land. This infighting between the Crusaders is why many historians hold the view that the Crusades were simply a front for Europe to invade the Holy Land for economic gain in the name of the Church. Another factor contributing to this theory is that while the army of crusaders marched towards Jerusalem they pillaged the land as they went. The church and feudal Lords vowing to return the land to its original beauty, and inhabitants, this rarely happened though, as the Lords often kept the land for themselves. A full 800 years after the Crusades, Pope John Paul II expressed his sorrow for the massacre of innocent people and the lasting damage that the Medieval church caused in that area of the World.

1. What is the tone of this article?

   a. Subjective
   b. Objective
   c. Persuasive
   d. None of the Above

2. What can all historians agree on concerning the Crusades?

   a. It achieved great things
   b. It stabilized the Holy Land
   c. It was bloody and brutal
   d. It helped defend Europe from the Byzantine Empire

3. What impact did the feudal system have on the Crusades?

   a. It unified the Crusaders
   b. It helped gather volunteers
   c. It had no effect on the Crusades
   d. It led to infighting, causing more damage than good

4. What does Saracen mean?

   a. Muslim
   b. Christian
   c. Knight
   d. Holy Land

Questions 5 - 8 refer to the following passage.

ABC Electric Warranty

ABC Electric Company warrants that its products are free from defects in material and workmanship. Subject to the conditions and limitations set forth below, ABC Electric will, at its option, either repair or replace any part of its products that prove defective due to improper workmanship or materials.

This limited warranty does not cover any damage to the product from improper installation, accident, abuse, misuse, natural disaster, insufficient or excessive electrical supply, abnormal mechanical or environmental conditions, or any unauthorized disassembly, repair, or modification.

This limited warranty also does not apply to any product on which the original identification information has been altered, or removed, has not been handled or packaged correctly, or has been sold as second-hand.

This limited warranty covers only repair, replacement, refund or credit for defective ABC Electric products, as provided above.

5. I tried to repair my ABC Electric blender, but could not, so can I get it repaired under this warranty?

    a. Yes, the warranty still covers the blender

    b. No, the warranty does not cover the blender

    c. Uncertain. ABC Electric may or may not cover repairs under this warranty

6. My ABC Electric fan is not working. Will ABC Electric provide a new one or repair this one?

    a. ABC Electric will repair my fan

    b. ABC Electric will replace my fan

    c. ABC Electric could either replace or repair my fan can request either a replacement or a repair.

Practice Test Questions 2

7. My stove was damaged in a flood. Does this warranty cover my stove?

    a. Yes, it is covered.

    b. No, it is not covered.

    c. It may or may not be covered.

    d. ABC Electric will decide if it is covered

8. Which of the following is an example of improper workmanship?

    a. Missing parts

    b. Defective parts

    c. Scratches on the front

    d. None of the above

Questions 9 – 12 refer to the following passage.

Passage 2 - Women and Advertising

Only in the last few generations have media messages been so widespread and so readily seen, heard, and read by so many people. Advertising is an important part of both selling and buying anything from soap to cereal to jeans. For whatever reason, more consumers are women than are men. Media message are subtle but powerful, and more attention has been paid lately to how these message affect women. Of all the products that women buy, makeup, clothes, and other stylistic or cosmetic products are among the most popular. This means that companies focus their advertising on women, promising them that their product will make her feel, look, or smell better than the next company's product will. This competition has resulted in advertising that is more and more ideal and less and less possible for everyday women. However, because women do look to these ideals and the products they represent as how they can potentially become, many women have developed unhealthy attitudes about themselves when they have failed to become those ideals.

In recent years, more companies have tried to change advertisements to be healthier for women. This includes featuring models of more sizes and addressing a huge outcry against unfair tools such as airbrushing and photo editing. There is debate about what the right balance between real and ideal is, because fashion is also considered art and some changes are made to purposefully elevate fashionable products and signify that they are creative, innovative, and the work of individual people. Artists want their freedom protected as much as women do, and advertising agencies are often caught in the middle.

Some claim that the companies who make these changes are not doing enough. Many people worry that there are still not enough models of different sizes and different ethnicities.

Some people claim that companies use this healthier type of advertisement not for the good of women, but because they would like to sell products to the women who are looking for these kinds of messages. This is also a hard balance to find: companies need to make money, and women need to feel respected.

While the focus of this change has been on women, advertising can also affect men, and this change will hopefully be a lesson on media for all consumers.

9. The second paragraph states that advertising focuses on women

    a. to shape what the ideal should be

    b. because women buy makeup

    c. because women are easily persuaded

    d. because of the types of products that women buy

10. According to the passage, fashion artists and female consumers are at odds because

   a. there is a debate going on and disagreement drives people apart

   b. both of them are trying to protect their freedom to do something

   c. artists want to elevate their products above the reach of women

   d. women are creative, innovative, individual people

11. The author uses the phrase "for whatever reason" in this passage to

   a. keep the focus of the paragraph on media messages and not on the differences between men and women

   b. show that the reason for this is unimportant

   c. argue that it is stupid that more women are consumers than men

   d. show that he or she is tired of talking about why media messages are important

12. This passage suggests that

   a. advertising companies are still working on making their messages better

   b. all advertising companies seek to be more approachable for women

   c. women are only buying from companies that respect them

   d. artists could stop producing fashionable products if they feel bullied

Questions 13 - 16 refer to the following passage.

FDR, the Treaty of Versailles, and the Fourteen Points

At the conclusion of World War I, those who had won the war and those who were forced to admit defeat welcomed the end of the war and expected that a peace treaty would be signed. The American president, Franklin D. Roosevelt, played an important part in proposing what the agreements should be and did so through his Fourteen Points.
World War I had begun in 1914 when an Austrian archduke was assassinated, leading to a domino effect that pulled the world's most powerful countries into war on a large scale. The war catalysed the creation and use of deadly weapons that had not previously existed, resulting in a great loss of soldiers on both sides of the fighting. More than 9 million soldiers were killed.

The United States agreed to enter the war right before it ended, and many believed that its decision to become finally involved brought on the end of the war. FDR made it very clear that the U.S. was entering the war for moral reasons and had an agenda focused on world peace. The Fourteen Points were individual goals and ideas (focused on peace, free trade, open communication, and self-reliance) that FDR wanted the power nations to strive for now that the war had ended. He was optimistic and had many ideas about what could be accomplished through, and during the post-war peace. However, FDR's fourteen points were poorly received when he presented them to the leaders of other world powers, many of whom wanted only to help their own countries and to punish the Germans for fueling the war, and they fell by the wayside. World War II was imminent, for Germany lost everything.

Some historians believe that the other leaders who participated in the Treaty of Versailles weren't receptive to the Fourteen Points because World War I was fought almost entirely on European soil, and the United States lost much less than did the other powers. FDR was in a unique position to determine the fate of the war, but doing it on his own terms did not help accomplish his goals. This is only one historical example of how the United State has tried to use its power as an important country, but found itself limited because of geological or ideological factors.

13. The main idea of this passage is that

a. World War I was unfair because no fighting took place in America

b. World War II happened because of the Treaty of Versailles

c. the power the United States has to help other countries also prevents it from helping other countries

d. Franklin D. Roosevelt was one of the United States' smartest presidents

14. According to the second paragraph, World War I started because

a. an archduke was assassinated

b. weapons that were more deadly had been developed

c. a domino effect of allies agreeing to help each other

d. the world's most powerful countries were large

15. The author includes the detail that 9 million soldiers were killed

a. to demonstrate why European leaders were hesitant to accept peace

b. to show the reader the dangers of deadly weapons

c. to make the reader think about which countries lost the most soldiers

d. to demonstrate why World War II was imminent

16. According to this passage, catalysed means

a. analyzed

b. sped up

c. invented

d. funded

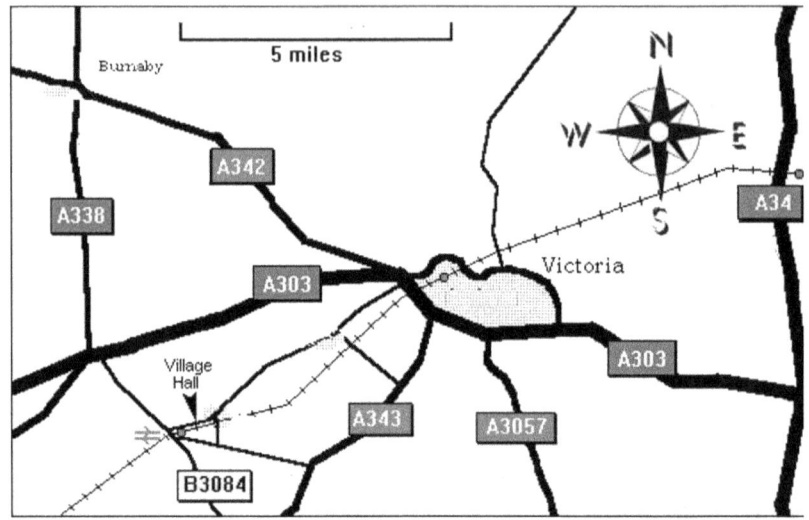

17. Approximately how far is Victoria to Burnaby?

    a. About 10 miles
    b. About 5 miles
    c. About 15 miles
    d. About 20 miles

18. How is the Village Hall from Victoria?

    a. About 10 miles
    b. About 5 miles
    c. About 15 miles
    d. About 20 miles

Questions 19 - 22 refer to the following passage.

Chocolate Chip Cookies

3/4 cup sugar
3/4 cup packed brown sugar
1 cup butter, softened
2 large eggs, beaten
1 teaspoon vanilla extract
2 1/4 cups all-purpose flour
1 teaspoon baking soda
3/4 teaspoon salt
2 cups semisweet chocolate chips
If desired, 1 cup chopped pecans, or chopped walnuts.
Preheat oven to 375 degrees.

Mix sugar, brown sugar, butter, vanilla and eggs in a large bowl. Stir in flour, baking soda, and salt. The dough will be very stiff.

Stir in chocolate chips by hand with a sturdy wooden spoon. Add the pecans, or other nuts, if desired. Stir until the chocolate chips and nuts are evenly dispersed.

Drop dough by rounded tablespoonfuls 2 inches apart onto a cookie sheet.

Bake 8 to 10 minutes, or, until light brown. Cookies may look underdone, but they will finish cooking after you take them out of the oven.

19. What is the correct order for adding these ingredients?

    a. Brown sugar, baking soda, chocolate chips
    b. Baking soda, brown sugar, chocolate chips
    c. Chocolate chips, baking soda, brown sugar
    d. Baking soda, chocolate chips, brown sugar

20. What does sturdy mean?

   a. Long
   b. Strong
   c. Short
   d. Wide

21. What does disperse mean?

   a. Scatter
   b. To form a ball
   c. To stir
   d. To beat

22. When can you stop stirring the nuts?

   a. When the cookies are cooked.
   b. When the nuts are evenly distributed.
   c. When the nuts are added.
   d. After the chocolate chips are added.

Questions 23 - 26 refer to the following passage.

Passage 5 - Frankenstein

Great God! What a scene has just taken place! I am yet dizzy with the remembrance of it. I hardly know whether I shall have the power to detail it; yet the tale which I have recorded would be incomplete without this final and wonderful catastrophe. I entered the cabin where lay the remains of my ill-fated and admirable friend. Over him hung a form which I cannot find words to describe—gigantic in stature, yet uncouth and distorted in its proportions. As he hung over the coffin, his face was concealed by long locks of ragged hair; but one vast hand was extended, in color and apparent texture like that of a mummy. When he heard the sound of my approach, he ceased to utter exclamations of grief and horror and sprung towards the window. Never did I behold a vision so horrible as his face, of such loathsome yet appalling hideousness. I shut my eyes involuntarily and endeavored to recollect what were my duties with regard to this destroyer. I called on him to stay.

He paused, looking on me with wonder, and again turning towards the lifeless form of his creator, he seemed to forget my presence, and every feature and gesture seemed instigated by the wildest rage of some uncontrollable passion.

"That is also my victim!" he exclaimed. "In his murder my crimes are consummated; the miserable series of my being is wound to its close! Oh, Frankenstein! Generous and self-devoted being! What does it avail that I now ask thee to pardon me? I, who irretrievably destroyed thee by destroying all thou lovedst. Alas! He is cold, he cannot answer me."

His voice seemed suffocated, and my first impulses, which had suggested to me the duty of obeying the dying request of my friend in destroying his enemy, were now suspended by a mixture of curiosity and compassion. I approached this tremendous being; I dared not again raise my eyes to his face, there was something so scaring and unearthly in his ugliness. I attempted to speak, but the words died away on my lips. The monster continued to utter wild and incoherent self-reproaches. At length I gathered resolution to address him in a pause of the tempest of his passion.

"Your repentance," I said, "is now superfluous. If you had listened to the voice of conscience and heeded the stings of remorse before you had urged your diabolical vengeance to this extremity, Frankenstein would yet have lived." [7]

23. Who is the "ill-fated and admirable friend" who is lying in the coffin?

    a. Frankenstein's monster
    b. Frankenstein
    c. Mary Shelley
    d. Unknown

24. Why is the speaker 'suspended" from following through on his duty to destroy the monster?

   a. The way the monster looks

   b. The monster's remorse

   c. Curiosity and compassion

   d. Fear the monster might kill him too

25. How does Frankenstein's monster destroy Frankenstein?

   a. By killing Frankenstein

   b. By letting himself be the monster everyone sees him as

   c. By destroying everything Frankenstein loved

   d. All of the above

26. When the Speaker says the monster's repentance is "superfluous, what does he mean?

   a. That it is unnecessary and unused because Frankenstein is already dead and cannot hear him

   b. That he accepts the repentance on behalf of Frankenstein

   c. That the monster does not actually feel remorseful

   d. That his repentance is unneeded because he did not do anything wrong

Questions 27 - 29 refer to the following passage.

Lowest Price Guarantee

Get it for less. Guaranteed!

ABC Electric will beat any advertised price by 10% of the difference.

   1) If you find a lower advertised price, we will beat it by 10% of the difference.

2) If you find a lower advertised price within 30 days* of your purchase we will beat it by 10% of the difference.

3) If our own price is reduced within 30 days* of your purchase, bring in your receipt and we will refund the difference.

*14 days for computers, monitors, printers, laptops, tablets, cellular & wireless devices, home security products, projectors, camcorders, digital cameras, radar detectors, portable DVD players, DJ and pro-audio equipment, and air conditioners.

27. I bought a radar detector 15 days ago and saw an ad for the same model only cheaper. Can I get 10% of the difference refunded?

a. Yes. Since it is less than 30 days, you can get 10% of the difference refunded.

b. No. Since it is more than 14 days, you cannot get 10% of the difference re-funded.

c. It depends on the cashier.

d. Yes. You can get the difference refunded.

28. I bought a flat-screen TV for $500 10 days ago and found an advertisement for the same TV, at another store, on sale for $400. How much will ABC refund under this guarantee?

a. $100
b. $110
c. $10
d. $400

29. What is the purpose of this passage?

   a. To inform
   b. To educate
   c. To persuade
   d. To entertain

Questions 30 refers to the following passage.

Passage 6 - What Is Mardi Gras?

Mardi Gras is fast becoming one of the South's most famous and most celebrated holidays. The word Mardi Gras comes from the French and the literal translation is "Fat Tuesday." The holiday has also been called Shrove Tuesday, due to its associations with Lent. The purpose of Mardi Gras is to celebrate and enjoy before the Lenten season of fasting and repentance begins.

What originated by the French Explorers in New Orleans, Louisiana in the 17th century is now celebrated all over the world. Panama, Italy, Belgium and Brazil all host large scale Mardi Gras celebrations, and many smaller cities and towns celebrate this fun loving Tuesday as well. Usually held in February or early March, Mardi Gras is a day of extravagance, a day for people to eat, drink and be merry, to wear costumes, masks and to dance to jazz music.
The French explorers on the Mississippi River would be in shock today if they saw the opulence of the parades and floats that grace the New Orleans streets during Mardi Gras these days. Parades in New Orleans are divided by organizations. These are more commonly known as Krewes.

Being a member of a Krewe is quite a task because Krewes are responsible for overseeing the parades. Each Krewe's parade is ruled by a Mardi Gras "King and Queen." The role of the King and Queen is to "bestow" gifts on their adoring fans as the floats ride along the street. They throw doubloons, which is fake money and usually colored green, purple and gold, which are the colors of Mardi Gras. Beads in those color shades are also thrown and cups are thrown as well. Beads are by far the most popular souvenir of any Mardi Gras parade, with each spectator attempting to gather as many as possible.

30. The purpose of Mardi Gras is to

    a. Repent for a month.
    b. Celebrate in extravagant ways.
    c. Be a member of a Krewe.
    d. Explore the Mississippi.

MATHEMATICS

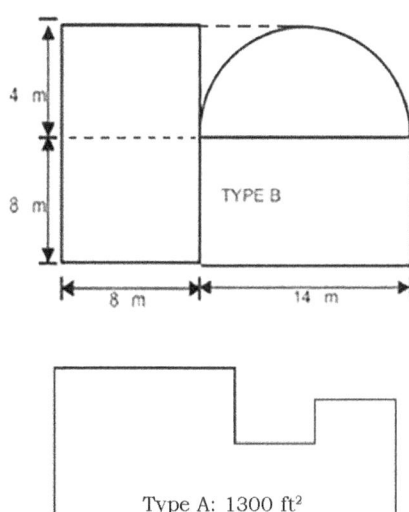

1. The price of houses in a certain subdivision is based on the total area. Susan is watching her budget and wants to choose the house with the lowest area. Which house type, A (1300 ft2) or B, should she choose if she would like the house with the lowest price?
($1 cm^2 = 4.0 ft^2$ & $\pi = 22/7$)

   a. Type B is smaller 140 ft²
   b. Type A is smaller
   c. Type B is smaller at 855 ft²
   d. Type B is larger

2. Using the quadratic formula, solve the quadratic equation: $0.9x^2 + 1.8x - 2.7 = 0$

   a. 1 and 3
   b. -3 and 1
   c. -3 and -1
   d. -1 and 3

3. Subtract polynomials $4x^3 - 2x^2 - 10$ and $5x^3 + x^2 + x + 5$.

   a. $-x^3 - 3x^2 - x - 15$
   b. $9x^3 - 3x^2 - x - 15$
   c. $-x^3 - x^2 + x - 5$
   d. $9x^3 - x^2 + x + 5$

4. Find x and y from the following system of equations:

$(4x + 5y)/3 = ((x - 3y)/2) + 4$
$(3x + y)/2 = ((2x + 7y)/3) - 1$

   a. (1, 3)
   b. (2, 1)
   c. (1, 1)
   d. (0, 1)

Practice Test Questions 2

5. Using the factoring method, solve the quadratic equation: $x^2 + 12x - 13 = 0$

    a. -13 and 1
    b. -13 and -1
    c. 1 and 13
    d. -1 and 13

6. Using the quadratic formula, solve the quadratic equation:

$$\frac{x+2}{x-2} + \frac{x-2}{x+2} = 0$$

    a. It has infinite numbers of solutions
    b. 0 and 1
    c. It has no solutions
    d. 0

7. Turn the following expression into a simple polynomial:

$5(3x^2 - 2) - x^2(2 - 3x)$

    a. $3x^3 + 17x^2 - 10$
    b. $3x^3 + 13x^2 + 10$
    c. $-3x^3 - 13x^2 - 10$
    d. $3x^3 + 13x^2 - 10$

8. Solve $(x^3 + 2)(x^2 - x) - x^5$.

    a. $2x^5 - x^4 + 2x^2 - 2x$
    b. $-x^4 + 2x^2 - 2x$
    c. $-x^4 - 2x^2 - 2x$
    d. $-x^4 + 2x^2 + 2x$

9. $9ab^2 + 8ab^2 =$

   a. ab^2
   b. $17ab^2$
   c. 17
   d. $17a^2b^2$

10. **Factor the polynomial** $x^2 - 7x - 30$.

   a. $(x + 15)(x - 2)$
   b. $(x + 10)(x - 3)$
   c. $(x - 10)(x + 3)$
   d. $(x - 15)(x + 2)$

11. **If a and b are real numbers, solve the following equation:** $(a + 2)x - b = -2 + (a + b)x$

   a. -1
   b. 0
   c. 1
   d. 2

12. **If** $A = -2x^4 + x^2 - 3x$, $B = x^4 - x^3 + 5$ **and** $C = x^4 + 2x^3 + 4x + 5$, **find** $A + B - C$.

   a. $x^3 + x^2 + x + 10$
   b. $-3x^3 + x^2 - 7x + 10$
   c. $-2x^4 - 3x^3 + x^2 - 7x$
   d. $-3x^4 + x^3 + x^2 - 7x$

13. $(4Y^3 - 2Y^2) + (7Y^2 + 3y - y) =$

   a. $4y^3 + 9y^2 + 4y$
   b. $5y^3 + 5y^2 + 3y$
   c. $4y^3 + 7y^2 + 2y$
   d. $4y^3 + 5y^2 + 2y$

14. Turn the following expression into a simple polynomial: $1 - x(1 - x(1 - x))$

    a. $x^3 + x^2 - x + 1$

    b. $-x^3 - x^2 + x + 1$

    c. $-x^3 + x^2 - x + 1$

    d. $x^3 + x^2 - x - 1$

15. $7(2y + 8) + 1 - 4(y + 5) =$

    a. $10y + 36$

    b. $10y + 77$

    c. $18y + 37$

    d. $10y + 37$

16. Richard gives 's' amount of salary to each of his 'n' employees weekly. If he has 'x' amount of money then how many days he can employ these 'n' employees.

    a. $sx/7n$

    b. $7x/nx$

    c. $nx/7s$

    d. $7x/ns$

17. Factor the polynomial $x^2 - 3x - 4$.

    a. $(x + 1)(x - 4)$

    b. $(x - 1)(x + 4)$

    c. $(x - 1)(x - 4)$

    d. $(x + 1)(x + 4)$

18. Solve the inequality: $(2x + 1)/(2x - 1) < 1$.

   a. $(-2, +\infty)$
   b. $(1, +\infty)$
   c. $(-\infty, -2)$
   d. $(-\infty, 1/2)$

19. Using the quadratic formula, solve the quadratic equation:

$(a^2 - b^2)x^2 + 2ax + 1 = 0$

   a. $a/(a + b)$ and $b/(a + b)$
   b. $1/(a + b)$ and $a/(a + b)$
   c. $a/(a + b)$ and $a/(a - b)$
   d. $-1/(a + b)$ and $-1/(a - b)$

20. Turn the following expression into a simple polynomial: $(a + b)(x + y) + (a - b)(x - y) - (ax + by)$

   a. $ax + by$
   b. $ax - by$
   c. $ax^2 + by^2$
   d. $ax^2 - by^2$

21. Given polynomials $A = 4x^5 - 2x^2 + 3x - 2$ and $B = -3x^4 - 5x^2 - 4x + 5$, find $A + B$.

   a. $x^5 - 3x^2 - x - 3$
   b. $4x^5 - 3x^4 + 7x^2 + x + 3$
   c. $4x^5 - 3x^4 - 7x^2 - x + 3$
   d. $4x^5 - 3x^4 - 7x^2 - x - 7$

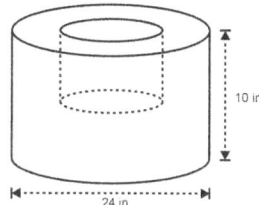

Note: figure not drawn to scale

22. What is the volume of the above solid made by a hollow cylinder that is half the size (in all dimensions) of the larger cylinder?

    a. 1440 π in³
    b. 1260 π in³
    c. 1040 π in³
    d. 960 π in³

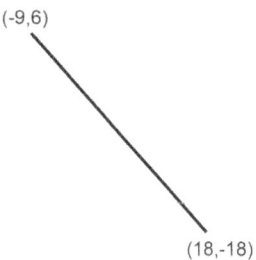

23. What is the slope of the line above?

    a. -8/9
    b. 9/8
    c. -9/8
    d. 8/9

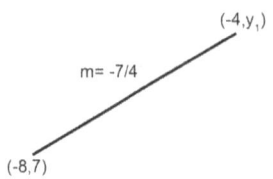

24. With the data given above, what is the value of y_1?

    a. 0
    b. -7
    c. 7
    d. 8

25. The area of a rectangle is 20 cm². If one side increases by 1 cm and other by 2 cm, the area of the new rectangle is 35 cm². Find the sides of the original rectangle.

    a. (4,8)
    b. (4,5)
    c. (2.5,8)
    d. b and c

26. What is the distance between the two points?

    a. ≈19
    b. 22
    c. ≈21
    d. ≈20

27. Find the solution for the following linear equation:
1/(4x - 2) = 5/6

    a. 0.2
    b. 0.4
    c. 0.6
    d. 0.8

28. How much water can be stored in a cylindrical container 5 meters in diameter and 12 meters high?

Note: figure not drawn to scale

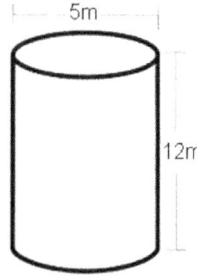

    a. 235.65 m³
    b. 223.65 m³
    c. 240.65 m³
    d. 252.65 m³

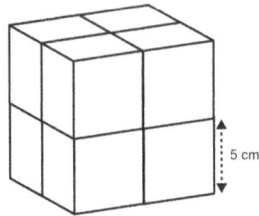

Note: figure not drawn to scale

29. Assuming the figure above has cubes, what is the volume?

    a. 125 cm³
    b. 875 cm³
    c. 1000 cm³
    d. 500 cm³

30. Solve

$x\sqrt{5} - y = \sqrt{5}$
$x - y\sqrt{5} = 5$

    a. $(0, -\sqrt{5})$
    b. $(0, \sqrt{5})$
    c. $(-\sqrt{5}, 0)$
    d. $(\sqrt{5}, 0)$

WRITING

Directions: Choose the word or phrase that best completes the sentence.

1. ____ won first place in the Western Division?

   a. Whom
   b. Which
   c. What
   d. Who

2. There are now several ways to listen to music, including radio, CDs, and Mp3 files ____ you can download onto an MP3 player.

   a. on which
   b. who
   c. whom
   d. which

3. As the tallest monument in the United States, the St. Louis Arch ____ to an impressive 630 feet.

   a. has rose
   b. is risen
   c. rises
   d. No change is necessary.

4. The tired, old woman should ____ on the sofa.

   a. lie
   b. lays
   c. laid
   d. None of the options are correct.

5. Did the students understand that Thanksgiving always _____ on the fourth Thursday in November?

    a. None of the options are correct.
    b. falling
    c. has fell
    d. falls

6. Collecting stamps, _____ models, and listening to shortwave radio were Rick's main hobbies.

    a. building
    b. build
    c. having built
    d. None of the options are correct.

7. Every morning, after the kids _____ for school and before the sun came up, my mother makes herself a cup of cocoa.

    a. had left
    b. leave
    c. have left
    d. None of the options are correct.

8. Elaine promised to bring the camera _____ at the mall yesterday.

    a. by me
    b. with me
    c. at me
    d. to me

Practice Test Questions 2

9. Last night, he _____ the sleeping bag down beside my mattress.

   a. lay
   b. lain
   c. has laid
   d. laid

10. I would have bought the shirt for you if _____ you liked it.

   a. had known
   b. have known
   c. would know
   d. None of the options are correct.

11. Until you _____ the overdue books to the library, you can't take any new ones home.

   a. take
   b. bring
   c. None of the choices are correct.

12. If they had gone to the party, he would _____ too.

   a. gone
   b. went
   c. have went
   d. had went

13. His doctor suggested that he eat _____ snacks and do less lounging on the couch.

    a. less

    b. fewer

    c. None of the choices are correct.

14. His father is _____.

    a. a poet and novelist

    b. a poet and a novelist

    c. either of the above

    d. none of the above

15. Choose the sentence with the correct punctuation.

    a. George wrecked John's car that was the end of their friendship.

    b. George wrecked John's car. that was the end of their friendship.

    c. The sentence is correct.

    d. None of the choices are correct.

16. Choose the sentence with the correct punctuation.

    a. The dress was not Gina's favorite; however, she wore it to the dance.

    b. None of the choices are correct.

    c. The dress was not Gina's favorite, however; she wore it to the dance.

    d. The dress was not Gina's favorite however, she wore it to the dance.

17. Choose the sentence with the correct punctuation.

a. Chris showed his dedication to golf in many ways, for example, he watched all of the tournaments on television.

b. The sentence is correct.

c. Chris showed his dedication to golf in many ways, for example; he watched all of the tournaments on television.

d. Chris showed his dedication to golf in many ways for example he watched all of the tournaments on television.

18. Choose the sentence with the correct grammar.

a. If Joe had told me the truth, I wouldn't have been so angry.
b. If Joe would have told me the truth, I wouldn't have been so angry.
c. I wouldn't have been so angry if Joe would have told the truth.
d. If Joe would have telled me the truth, I wouldn't have been so angry.

19. Choose the sentence with the correct punctuation.

a. I can never remember how to use those two common words, "sell," meaning to trade a product for money, or sale- meaning an event where products are traded for less money than usual.

b. I can never remember how to use those two common words, "sell," meaning to trade a product for money, or "sale," meaning an event where products are traded for less money than usual.

c. I can never remember how to use those two common words, "sell," meaning to trade a product for money, or sale, meaning an event where products are traded for less money than usual.

d. None of the above are correct.

20. Choose the sentence with the correct punctuation.

a. The class just finished reading, -"Leinengen versus the Ants," a short story by Carl Stephenson about a plantation owner's battle with army ants.

b. The class just finished reading, Leinengen versus the Ants, a short story by Carl Stephenson about a plantation owner's battle with army ants.

c. The class just finished reading, "Leinengen versus the Ants," a short story by Carl Stephenson about a plantation owner's battle with army ants.

d. None of the above

21. Choose the sentence with the correct punctuation.

a. My best friend said, "always count your change."

b. My best friend said, "<u>Always Count your Change</u>."

c. My best friend said, "Always count your change."

d. None of the choices are correct.

22. Choose the sentence that is written correctly.

a. He told him to rise it up

b. He told him to raise it up

c. Either of the above

d. None of the above

23. Choose the sentence that is written correctly.

a. I shall arrive early and I will have breakfast with you

b. I shall arrive early and I would have breakfast with you

c. I shall arrive early and have breakfast with you.

d. None of the above

Practice Test Questions 2

24. Choose the sentence that is written correctly.

a. The gold coins with the diamonds is to be seized
b. The gold coins with the diamonds are to be seized.
c. None of the above

25. Choose the sentence that is written correctly.

a The trousers are to be delivered today
b. The trousers is to be delivered today.
c. Both of the above

26. Choose the sentence that is written correctly.

a. She was nodding her head, her hips are swaying.
b. She was nodding her head, her hips is swaying.
c. She was nodding her head, her hips were swaying.
d. None of the above

27. Choose the sentence that is written correctly.

a. The sad news were delivered this morning
b. The sad news are delivered this morning.
c. The sad news was delivered this morning
d. None of the above

28. Choose the sentence that is written correctly.

a. The sentence is correct
b. Mathematics are my best subject in school
c. Mathematics was my best subject in school
d. Mathematics were my best subject in school.

29. Choose the sentence that is written correctly.

a. 15 minutes is all the time you have to complete the test.

b. 15 minutes are all the time you have to complete the test.

c. Both of the above.

d. None of the above.

30. Choose the sentence that is written correctly.

a. Everyone are to wear a black tie.

b. Everyone have to wear a black tie.

c. Everyone has to wear a black tie.

d. None of the above.

Answer Key

Reading Comprehension

1. A
Choice B is incorrect; the author did not express their opinion on the subject matter. Choice C is incorrect, the author was not trying to prove a point, nor is the author trying to persuade.

2. C
Choice C is correct; historians believe it was brutal and bloody. Choice A is incorrect; there is no consensus that the Crusades achieved great things. Choice B is incorrect; it did not stabilize the Holy Lands. Choice D is incorrect, some historians do believe this was the purpose but not all historians.

3. D
The feudal system led to infighting. Choice A is incorrect, it had the opposite effect. Choice B is incorrect, though this is a good answer, it is not the best answer. The Church asked for volunteers not the Feudal Lords. Choice C is incorrect, it did have an effect on the Crusades.

4. A
Saracen was a generic term for Muslims widely used in Europe during the later medieval era.

5. B
This warranty does not cover a product that you have tried to fix yourself. From paragraph two, "This limited warranty does not cover ... any unauthorized disassembly, repair, or modification. "

6. C
ABC Electric could either replace or repair the fan, provided the other conditions are met. ABC Electric has the option to repair or replace.

7. B
The warranty does not cover a stove damaged in a flood. From the passage, "This limited warranty does not cover any damage to the product from improper installation, accident, abuse, misuse, natural disaster, insufficient or excessive electrical supply, abnormal mechanical or environmental conditions."

A flood is an "abnormal environmental condition," and a natural disaster, so it is not covered.

8. A
A missing part is an example of defective workmanship. This is an error made in the manufacturing process. A defective part is not considered workmanship.

9. D
This question tests the reader's summarization skills. The other choices A, B, and C focus on portions of the second paragraph that are too narrow and do not relate to the specific portion of text in question. The complexity of the sentence may mislead students into selecting one of these answers, but rearranging or restating the sentence will lead the reader to the correct answer. In addition, choice A makes an assumption that may or may not be true about the intentions of the company, choice B focuses on one product rather than the idea of the products, and choice C makes an assumption about women that may or may not be true and is not supported by the text.

10. B
This question tests reader's attention to detail. If a reader selects A, he or she may have picked up on the use of the word "debate" and assumed, very logically, that the two are at odds because they are fighting; however, this is simply not supported in the text. Choice C also uses very specific quotes from the text, but it rearranges and gives them false meaning. The artists want to elevate their creations above the creations of other artists, thereby showing that they are "creative" and "innovative." Similarly, choice D takes phrases straight from the text and rearranges and confuses them. The artists are described as wanting to be "creative, innovative, individual people," not the women.

11. A
This question tests reader's vocabulary and summarization skills. This phrase, used by the author, may seem flippant and dismissive if readers focus on the word "whatever" and misinterpret it as a popular, colloquial term. In this way, choices B and C may mislead the reader to selecting one of them by including the terms "unimportant" and "stupid," respectively. Choice D is a similar misreading, but doesn't make sense when the phrase is at the beginning of the passage and the entire passage is on media messages. Choice A is literally and contextually appropriate, and the reader can understand that the author would like to keep the introduction focused on the topic the passage is going to discuss.

12. A
This question tests a reader's inference skills. The extreme use of the word "all" in choice B suggests that every single advertising company are working to be approachable, and while this is not only unlikely, the text specifically states that "more" companies have done this, signifying that they have not all participated, even if it's a possibility that they may some day. The use of the limiting word "only" in choice C lends that answer similar problems; women are still buying from companies who do not care about this message, or those companies would not be in business, and the passage specifies that "many" women are worried about media messages, but not all. Readers may find choice D logical, especially if they are looking to make an inference, and while this may be a possibility, the passage does not suggest or discuss this happening. Choice A is correct based on specifically because of the relation between "still working" in the answer and "will hopefully" and the extensive discussion on companies struggles, which come only with progress, in the text.

13. C
This question tests the reader's summarization skills. The entire passage is leading up to the idea that the president of the US may not have had grounds to assert his Fourteen Points when other countries had lost so much. Choice A is pretty directly inferred by the text, but it does not adequately summarize what the entire passage is trying to communicate. Choice B may also be inferred by the passage when it says that the war is "imminent," but it does not represent the entire message, either. The passage does seem to be in praise of FDR, or at least in respect of him, but it does not

in any way claim that he is the smartest president, nor does this represent the many other points included. Choice C is then the obvious answer, and most directly relates to the closing sentences which it rewords.

14. C
This question tests the reader's attention to detail. The passage does state that choices A and B are true, and while those statements are in proximity to the explanation for why the war started, they are not the reason given. Choice D is a mix up of words used in the passage, which says that the largest powers were in play but not that this fact somehow started the war. The passage does make a direct statement that a domino effect started the war, supporting choice C as the correct answer.

15. A
This question tests the reader's understanding of functions in writing. Throughout the passage, it states that leaders of other nations were hesitant to accept generous or peaceful terms because of the grievances of the war, and the great loss of life was chief among these. While the passage does touch on the devastation of deadly weapons (B), the use of this raw, emotional fact serves a much larger purpose, and the focus of the passage is not the weapons. While readers may indeed consider who lost the most soldiers (C) when, so many countries were involved and the inequalities of loss are mentioned in the passage, there is no discussion of this in the passage. Choice D is related to A, but choice A is more direct and relates more to the passage.

16. B
This question tests the reader's vocabulary skills. Choice A may seem appealing to readers because it is phonetically similar to "catalysed," but the two are not related in any other way. Choice C makes sense in context, but if plugged in to the sentence creates a redundancy that doesn't make sense. Choice D does also not make sense contextually, even if the reader may consider that funds were needed to create more weaponry, especially if it was advanced.

Practice Test Questions 2

17. A
Victoria is about 5 miles from Burnaby.

18. B
The Village Hall is about 5 miles from Victoria.

19. A
The correct order of ingredients is brown sugar, baking soda and chocolate chips.

20. B
Sturdy: strong, solid in structure or person. In context, Stir in chocolate chips by hand with a *sturdy* wooden spoon.

21. A
Disperse: to scatter in different directions or break up. In context, Stir until the chocolate chips and nuts are evenly *dispersed*.

22. B
You can stop stirring the nuts when they are evenly distributed. From the passage, "Stir until the chocolate chips and nuts are evenly dispersed."

23. B
Choice A is incorrect as the Monster killed Frankenstein, not the other way around. Choice B is correct, Frankenstein is dead. Choice C is incorrect - Mary Shelley is the author. Choice D is incorrect, the person is called Frankenstein.

24. C
The speaker 'suspended' from following through on his duty to destroy the monster due to curiosity and compassion. The other choices may seem reasonable, but are not explicitly given in the passage.

25. D
All the choices are correct. Frankenstein's monster destroys Frankenstein by

    a. By killing Frankenstein

    b. By letting himself be the monster everyone sees him as

c. By destroying everything Frankenstein loved

26. A
Superfluous means unnecessary. Looking at the context of the word as it is used in the passage:

"Your repentance," I said, "is now superfluous. If you had listened to the voice of conscience and heeded the stings of remorse before you had urged your diabolical vengeance to this extremity, Frankenstein would yet have lived."

27. B
The time limit for radar detectors is 14 days. Since you made the purchase 15 days ago, you do not qualify for the guarantee.

28. B
Since you made the purchase 10 days ago, you are covered by the guarantee. Since it is an advertised price at a different store, ABC Electric will "beat" the price by 10% of the difference, which is,

500 – 400 = 100 – difference in price

100 X 10% = $10 – 10% of the difference

The advertised lower price is $400. ABC will beat this price by 10% so they will refund $100 + 10 = $110.

29. C
The purpose of this passage is to persuade.

30. B
The correct answer can be found in the fourth sentence of the first paragraph.

Choice A is incorrect because repenting begins the day AFTER Mardi Gras. Choice C is incorrect because you can celebrate Mardi Gras without being a member of a Krewe.

Choice D is incorrect because exploration does not play any role in a modern Mardi Gras celebration.

MATHEMATICS

1. D
Area of Type B consists of two rectangles and a half circle. We can find these three areas and sum them up to find the total area:

Area of the left rectangle: $(4 + 8) * 8 = 96$ m²

Area of the right rectangle: $14 * 8 = 112$ m²

The diameter of the circle is equal to 14 m. So, the radius is $14/2 = 7$:

Area of the half circle = $(1/2) * \pi r^2 = (1/2) * (22/7) * (7)^2 = (1 * 22 * 49)/(2 * 7) = 77$ m²

Area of Type B = $96 + 112 + 77 = 285$ m²

Converting this area to ft²: 285 m² = 285 * 10.76 ft² = 3066.6 ft²

Type B is (3066.6 - 1300 = 1766.6 ft²) 1766.6 ft² larger than type A.

2. B
To solve the equation, we need the equation in the form $ax^2 + bx + c = 0$.

$0.9x^2 + 1.8x - 2.7 = 0$ is already in this form.

The quadratic formula to find the roots of a quadratic equation is:

$x_{1,2} = (-b \pm \sqrt{\Delta}) / 2a$ where $\Delta = b^2 - 4ac$ and is called the discriminant of the quadratic equation.

In our question, the equation is $0.9x^2 + 1.8x - 2.7 = 0$. To eliminate the decimals, let us multiply the equation by 10:

$9x^2 + 18x - 27 = 0$ ... This equation can be simplified by 9 since each term contains 9:

$x^2 + 2x - 3 = 0$

By remembering the form $ax^2 + bx + c = 0$:

$a = 1, b = 2, c = -3$

So, we can find the discriminant first, and then the roots of the equation:

$\Delta = b^2 - 4ac = (2)^2 - 4 * 1 * (-3) = 4 + 12 = 16$

$x_{1,2} = (-b \pm \sqrt{\Delta}) / 2a = (-2 \pm \sqrt{16}) / 2 = (-2 \pm 4) / 2$

This means that the roots are,

$x_1 = (-2 - 4)/2 = -3$ and $x_2 = (-2 + 4)/2 = 1$

4. C
First, we need to arrange the two equations to obtain the form $ax + by = c$. We see that there are 3 and 2 in the denominators of both equations. If we equate all at 6, then we can cancel all 6 in the denominators and have straight equations:

Equate all denominators at 6:

$2(4x + 5y)/6 = 3(x - 3y)/6 + 4 * 6/6$ ... Now we can cancel 6 in the denominators:

$8x + 10y = 3x - 9y + 24$ ... We can collect x and y terms on left side of the equation:

$8x + 10y - 3x + 9y = 24$

$5x + 19y = 24$ ... Equation (I)

Let us arrange the second equation:

$3(3x + y)/6 = 2(2x + 7y)/6 - 1 * 6/6$ ... Now we can cancel 6 in the denominators:

$9x + 3y = 4x + 14y - 6$ ... We can collect x and y terms on left side of the equation:

$9x + 3y - 4x - 14y = -6$

5x - 11y = -6 ... Equation (II)

Now, we have two equations and two unknowns x and y. By writing the two equations one under the other and operating, we can find one unknowns first, and find the other next:

$\quad$ 5x + 19y = 24

-1/ 5x - 11y = -6 ... If we substitute this equation from the upper one, 5x cancels -5x:

$\quad$ 5x + 19y = 24

$\quad$ -5x + 11y = 6 ... Summing side-by-side:

$\quad$ 5x - 5x + 19y + 11y = 24 + 6

$\quad$ 30y = 30 ... Dividing both sides by 30:

$\quad$ y = 1

Inserting y = 1 into either of the equations, we can find the value of x. Choosing equation I:

5x + 19 * 1 = 24

5x = 24 - 19

5x = 5 ... Dividing both sides by 5:

x = 1

So, x = 1 and y = 1 is the solution; it is shown as (1, 1).

5. A
x^2 + 12x - 13 = 0 ... We try to separate the middle term 12x to find common factors with x^2 and -13 separately:

x^2 + 13x - x - 13 = 0 ... Here, we see that x is a common factor for x^2 and 13x, and -1 is a common factor for -x and -13:

x(x + 13) - 1(x + 13) = 0 ... Here, we have x times x + 13 and -1 times x + 13 summed up. This means that we have x - 1 times x + 13:

(x - 1)(x + 13) = 0

This is true when either or, both of the expressions in the parenthesis are equal to zero:

$x - 1 = 0$ ... $x = 1$

$x + 13 = 0$ ... $x = -13$

1 and -13 are the solutions for this quadratic equation.

6. C
This equation has no solution.

$x^2 + 4x + 4 + x^2 - 4x + 4 \;/\; (x - 2)(x + 2) = 0$

$2x^2 + 8 \;/\; (x - 2)(x + 2) = 0 \;\Rightarrow\; 2x^2 + 8 = 0$
$x^2 + 4 = 0$
$x_{1,2} = 0 \pm \sqrt{-4 * 4} \;/\; 2$
$x_{1,2} = 0 \pm \sqrt{-16} \;/\; 2$
Solution for the square root of -16 is not a real number, so this equation has no solution.

7. D
We need to distribute the factors to the terms inside the related parenthesis:

$5(3x^2 - 2) - x^2(2 - 3x) = 15x^2 - 10 - (2x^2 - 3x^3)$

$= 15x^2 - 10 - 2x^2 + 3x^3$

$= 3x^3 + 15x^2 - 2x^2 - 10$ ... similar terms written together to ease summing/substituting.

$= 3x^3 + 13x^2 - 10$

8. B
We need to distribute the factors to the terms inside the related parenthesis:

$(x^3 + 2)(x^2 - x) - x^5 = x^5 - x^4 + (2x^2 - 2x) - x^5$

$= x^5 - x^4 + 2x^2 - 2x - x^5$

$= x^5 - x^5 - x^4 + 2x^2 - 2x$ ... similar terms written together to ease summing/substituting.

$= -x^4 + 2x^2 - 2x$

9. B
To simplify the expression, we need to find common factors. We see that both terms contain the term ab^2. So, we can

take this term out of each term as a factor:
$ab^2(9 + 8) = 17ab^2$

10. C
$x^2 - 7x - 30 = 0$ ... We try to separate the middle term $-7x$ to find common factors with x^2 and -30 separately:

$x^2 - 10x + 3x - 30 = 0$ ... Here, we see that x is a common factor for x^2 and $-10x$, and 3 is a common factor for $3x$ and -30:

$x(x - 10) + 3(x - 10) = 0$ ... Here, we have x times $x - 10$ and 3 times $x - 10$ summed up. This means that we have $x + 3$ times $x - 10$:

$(x + 3)(x - 10) = 0$ or $(x - 10)(x + 3) = 0$

11. A
We need to simplify the equation by distributing factors and then collecting x terms on one side, and the others on the other side:

$(a + 2)x - b = -2 + (a + b)x$

$ax + 2x - b = -2 + ax + bx$

$ax + 2x - ax - bx = -2 + b$ ... ax and -ax cancel:

$2x - bx = -2 + b$ ... we take -1 as a factor on the right side:

$(2 - b)x = -(2 - b)$

$x = -(2 - b)/(2 - b)$ ... Simplifying by $2 - b$:

$x = -1$

12. C
We are asked to find $A + B - C$. By paying attention to the sign distribution; we write the polynomials and operate:

$A + B - C = (-2x^4 + x^2 - 3x) + (x^4 - x^3 + 5) - (x^4 + 2x^3 + 4x + 5)$

$= -2x^4 + x^2 - 3x + x^4 - x^3 + 5 - x^4 - 2x^3 - 4x - 5$

$= -2x^4 + x^4 - x^4 - x^3 - 2x^3 + x^2 - 3x - 4x + 5 - 5$ ... similar terms written together to ease summing/substituting.

$= -2x^4 - 3x^3 + x^2 - 7x$

13. D
To simplify, we remove parenthesis:

$(4y^3 - 2y^2) + (7y^2 + 3y - y) = 4y^3 - 2y^2 + 7y^2 + 3y - y$ ... Then, we operate within similar terms:

$= 4y^3 + (-2 + 7)y^2 + (3 - 1)y = 4y^3 + 5y^2 + 2y$

14. C
To obtain a polynomial, we should remove the parenthesis by distributing the related factors to the terms inside the parenthesis:

$1 - x(1 - x(1 - x)) = 1 - x(1 - (x - x * x)) = 1 - x(1 - x + x^2)$

$= 1 - (x - x * x + x * x^2) = 1 - x + x^2 - x^3$ ... Writing this result in descending order of powers:

$= -x^3 + x^2 - x + 1$

15. D
To simplify the expression, remove the parenthesis by distributing the related factors to the terms inside the parenthesis:

$7(2y + 8) + 1 - 4(y + 5) = (7 * 2y + 7 * 8) + 1 - (4 * y + 4 * 5)$

$= 14y + 56 + 1 - 4y - 20$

$= 14y - 4y + 56 + 1 - 20$ ... similar terms written together to ease summing/substituting.

$= 10y + 37$

16. D
We understand that each of the n employees earn s amount of salary weekly. This means that one employee earns s salary weekly. So; Richard has ns amount of money to employ n employees for a week.

We are asked to find the number of days n employees can be employed with x amount of money. We can do simple direct proportion:

If Richard can employ n employees for 7 days with ns amount of money,

Richard can employ n employees for y days with x amount of money ... y is the number of days we need to find.

Cross multiply:

y = (x * 7)/(ns)

y = 7x/ns

17. A
x^2 - 3x - 4 ... We try to separate the middle term -3x to find common factors with x^2 and -4 separately:

x^2 + x - 4x - 4 ... Here, we see that x is a common factor for x^2 and x, and -4 is a common factor for -4x and -4:

= x(x + 1) - 4(x + 1) ... Here, we have x times x + 1 and -4 times x + 1 summed up. This means that we have x - 4 times x + 1:

= (x - 4)(x + 1) or (x + 1)(x - 4)

18. D
We need to simplify and have x alone and on one side to solve the inequality:

(2x + 1)/(2x - 1) < 1

(2x + 1)/(2x - 1) - 1 < 0 ... We need to write the left side at the common denominator 2x - 1:

(2x + 1)/(2x - 1) - (2x - 1)/(2x - 1) < 0

(2x + 1 - 2x + 1)/(2x - 1) < 0 ... 2x and -2x terms cancel each other in the numerator:

2/(2x - 1) < 0

2 is a positive number; so,

2x - 1 < 0

2x < 1

$x < 1/2$ ... This means that x should be smaller than $1/2$ and not equal to $1/2$. This is shown as $(-\infty, 1/2)$.

19. D

To solve the equation, we need the equation in the form $ax^2 + bx + c = 0$.

$(a^2 - b^2)x^2 + 2ax + 1 = 0$ is already in this form.

The quadratic formula to find the roots of a quadratic equation is:

$x_{1,2} = (-b \pm \sqrt{\Delta}) / 2a$ where $\Delta = b^2 - 4ac$ and is called the discriminant of the quadratic equation.

In our question, the equation is $(a^2 - b^2)x^2 + 2ax + 1 = 0$.

By remembering the form $ax^2 + bx + c = 0$: $a = a^2 - b^2$, $b = 2a$, $c = 1$

So, we can find the discriminant first, and then the roots of the equation:

$\Delta = b^2 - 4ac = (2a)^2 - 4(a^2 - b^2) * 1 = 4a^2 - 4a^2 + 4b^2 = 4b^2$

$x_{1,2} = (-b \pm \sqrt{\Delta}) / 2a = (-2a \pm \sqrt{4b^2}) / (2(a^2 - b^2)) = (-2a \pm 2b) / (2(a^2 - b^2))$

$= 2(-a \pm b) / (2(a^2 - b^2))$ ... We can simplify by 2:

$= (-a \pm b) / (a^2 - b^2)$

This means that the roots are,

$x_1 = (-a - b) / (a^2 - b^2)$ ... $a^2 - b^2$ is two square differences:

$x_1 = -(a + b) / ((a - b)(a + b))$ ... $(a + b)$ terms cancel:

$x_1 = -1/(a - b)$

$x_2 = (-a + b) / (a^2 - b^2)$ ... $a^2 - b^2$ is two square differences:

$x_2 = -(a - b) / ((a - b)(a + b))$ ... $(a - b)$ terms cancel:

$x_2 = -1/(a + b)$

20. A

To simplify, we need to remove the parenthesis and see if any terms cancel:

$(a + b)(x + y) + (a - b)(x - y) - (ax + by) = ax + ay + bx + by + ax - ay - bx + by - ax - by$

By writing similar terms together:

$= ax + ax - ax + bx - bx + ay - ay + by + by - by$ ... + terms cancel - terms:

$= ax + by$

21. C

We are asked to add polynomials A + B. By paying attention to the sign distribution; we write the polynomials and operate:

$A + B = (4x^5 - 2x^2 + 3x - 2) + (-3x^4 - 5x^2 - 4x + 5)$

$= 4x^5 - 2x^2 + 3x - 2 - 3x^4 - 5x^2 - 4x + 5$ ... Writing similar terms together:

$= 4x^5 - 3x^4 - 2x^2 - 5x^2 + 3x - 4x - 2 + 5$ ... Operating within similar terms:

$= 4x^5 - 3x^4 - 7x^2 - x + 3$

22. B

Total Volume = Volume of large cylinder - Volume of small cylinder

Volume of a cylinder = area of base * height = $\pi r^2 * h$

Total Volume = $(\pi * 12^2 * 10) - (\pi * 6^2 * 5) = 1440\pi - 180\pi$

$= 1260\pi \text{ in}^3$

23. A

Slope (m) = change in y / change in x

If we know the coordinates of two points on a line, we can find the slope (m) with the below formula:

$m = (y_2 - y_1)/(x_2 - x_1)$ where (x_1, y_1) represent the coordinates of one point and (x_2, y_2) the other.

In this question:

$(-9, 6) : x_1 = -9, y_1 = 6$

$(18, -18) : x_2 = 18, y_2 = -18$

Inserting these values into the formula:

$m = (-18 - 6)/(18 - (-9)) = (-24)/(27)$ ... Simplifying by 3:

$m = -8/9$

24. A

If we know the coordinates of two points on a line, we can find the slope (m) with the below formula:
$m = (y_2 - y_1)/(x_2 - x_1)$ where (x_1, y_1) represent the coordinates of one point and (x_2, y_2) the other.

In this question:

$(-4, y_1) : x_1 = -4, y_1 =$ we will find

$(-8, 7) : x_2 = -8, y_2 = 7$

$m = -7/4$

Inserting these values into the formula:

$-7/4 = (7 - y_1)/(-8 - (-4))$

$-7/4 = (7 - y_1)/(-8 + 4)$

$7/(-4) = (7 - y_1)/(-4)$ ... Simplifying the denominators of both sides by -4:

$7 = 7 - y_1$

$0 = -y_1$

$y_1 = 0$

25. D

The area of a rectangle is found by multiplying the width to the length. If we call these sides with "a" and "b"; the area is $= a * b$.

We are given that $a * b = 20$ cm² ... Equation I

One side is increased by 1, and the other by 2 cm. So new side lengths are "a + 1" and "b + 2."

The new area is $(a + 1)(b + 2) = 35$ cm² ... Equation II

Using equations I and II, we can find a and b:

$ab = 20$

$(a + 1)(b + 2) = 35$ ... We need to distribute the terms in parenthesis:

$ab + 2a + b + 2 = 35$

We can insert $ab = 20$ to the above equation:

$20 + 2a + b + 2 = 35$

$2a + b = 35 - 2 - 20$

$2a + b = 13$ ... This is one equation with two unknowns. We need to use another information to have two equations with two unknowns which leads us to the solution. We know that $ab = 20$. So, we can use $a = 20/b$:

$2(20/b) + b = 13$

$40/b + b = 13$ ... We equate all denominators to "b" and eliminate it:

$40 + b^2 = 13b$

$b^2 - 13b + 40 = 0$ ... We can use the roots by factoring. We try to separate the middle term -13b to find common factors with b^2 and 40 separately:

$b^2 - 8b - 5b + 40 = 0$ ⋯ Here, we see that b is a common factor for b^2 and -8b, and -5 is a common factor for -5b and 40:

$b(b - 8) - 5(b - 8) = 0$ Here, we have b times b - 8 and -5 times b - 8 summed up. This means that we have b - 5 times b - 8:

$(b - 5)(b - 8) = 0$

This is true when either or both expressions in the parenthesis are equal to zero:

b - 5 = 0 ... b = 5

b - 8 = 0 ... b = 8

So we have two values for b, which means we have two values for a as well. To find a, we can use any equation we have. Let us use a = 20/b.

If b = 5, a = 20/b → a = 4

If b = 8, a = 20/b → a = 2.5

So, (a, b) pairs for the sides of the original rectangle are: (4, 5) and (2.5, 8). These are found in (b) and (c) answer choices.

26. D

The distance between two points is found by = $[(x_2 - x_1)^2 + (y_2 - y_1)^2]^{1/2}$

In this question:

(18, 12) : $x_1 = 18$, $y_1 = 12$

(9, -6) : $x_2 = 9$, $y_2 = -6$

Distance = $[(9 - 18)^2 + (-6 - 12)^2]^{1/2}$

$= [(-9)^2 + (-18)^2]^{1/2}$

$= (9^2 + 2^2 * 9^2)^{1/2}$

$= (9^2(1 + 5))^{1/2}$ ... We can take 9 out of the square root:

$= 9 * 6^{1/2}$

$= 9\sqrt{6}$

$= 9 * 2.45$

$= 22.04$

The distance is approximately 22 units.

27. D
$1/(4x - 2) = 5/6$ ... Cross multiply:
$5(4x - 2) = 1 * 6$ ... Now, we distribute 5 to the parenthesis:

$20x - 10 = 6$ ... We need x term alone on one side:

$20x = 6 + 10$

$20x = 16$ ... Dividing both sides by 20:

$x = 16/20$ ... Simplifying by 2, and 10 in the denominator gives the decimal equivalent of x:

$x = 8/10 = 0.8$

28. A
The formula of the volume of cylinder is the base area multiplied by the height. As the formula:

Volume of a cylinder = $\pi r^2 h$. Where π is 3.142, r is radius of the cross sectional area, and h is the height.

We know that the diameter is 5 meters, so the radius is 5/2 = 2.5 meters.

The volume is: V = $3.142 * 2.5^2 * 12 = 235.65$ m³.

29. C
The large cube is made up of 8 smaller cubes with 5 cm sides. The volume of a cube is found by the third power of

the length of one side.

Volume of the large cube = Volume of the small cube * 8

$= (5^3) * 8 = 125 * 8$

$= 1000 \text{ cm}^3$

There is another solution for this question. Find the side length of the large cube. There are two cubes rows with 5 cm length for each. So, one side of the large cube is 10 cm.

The volume of this large cube is equal to $10^3 = 1000 \text{ cm}^3$

30. A

First write the two equations one under the other. Our aim is to multiply equations with appropriate factors to eliminate one unknown and find the other, and then find the eliminated one using the found value.

$-\sqrt{5}$ / $x\sqrt{5} - y = \sqrt{5}$ ... If we multiply this equation by $\sqrt{5}$, y terms will cancel:

$\underline{x - y\sqrt{5} = 5}$

$-x\sqrt{5}\sqrt{5} + y\sqrt{5} = -\sqrt{5}\sqrt{5}$ ... using $\sqrt{5}\sqrt{5} = 5$:

$\underline{x - y\sqrt{5} = 5}$

$-5x + y\sqrt{5} = -5$

$\underline{x - y\sqrt{5} = 5}$ ... Summing side-by-side:

$-5x + y\sqrt{5} + x - y\sqrt{5} = -5 + 5$ ... $+ y\sqrt{5}$ and $- y\sqrt{5}$, -5 and $+ 5$ cancel:

$-4x = 0$

$x = 0$

Now, using either of the equations gives us the value of y. Let us choose equation 1:

$x\sqrt{5} - y = \sqrt{5}$

$0\sqrt{5} - y = \sqrt{5}$

$-y = \sqrt{5}$

$y = -\sqrt{5}$

The solution to the system is $(0, -\sqrt{5})$

WRITING

1. D
"Who" is correct because the question uses an active construction. "To whom was first place given?" is passive construction.

2. D
"Which" is correct, because the files are objects and not people.

3. C
The simple present tense, "rises," is correct.

4. A
"Lie" does not require a direct object, while "lay" does. The old woman might lie on the couch, which has no direct object, or she might lay the book down, which has the direct object, "the book."

5. D
The simple present tense, "falls," is correct because it is repeated action.

6. A
The present progressive, "building models," is correct in this sentence; it is required to match the other present progressive verbs.

7. C
Past Perfect tense describes a completed action in the past, before another action in the past.

8. D
The preposition "to" is the correct preposition to use with "bring."

9. D
"Laid" is the past tense.

10. A
This is a past unreal conditional sentence. It requires an 'if' clause and a result clause, and either clause can appear first. The 'if' clause uses the past perfect, while the result clause uses the past participle.

11. C
Bring vs. Take. Usage depends on your location. Something coming your way is brought to you. Something going away is taken from you.

12. A
The sentence is correct. Went vs. Gone. Went is the simple past tense. Gone is used in the past perfect.

13. B
Fewer vs. Less. 'Fewer' is used with count-ables and 'less' is used with uncount-ables.

14. B
His father is a poet and a novelist. It is necessary to use 'a' twice in this sentence for the two distinct things.

15. C
The semicolon links independent clauses. An independent clause can form a complete sentence by itself.

16. A
The semicolon links independent clauses with a conjunction (However).

17. B
The sentence is correct. The semicolon links independent clauses. An independent clause can form a complete sentence by itself.

18. A
The third conditional is used for talking about an unreal situation (that did not happen) in the past. For example, "If I had studied harder, [if clause] I would have passed the

exam [main clause]. Which is the same as, "I failed the exam, because I didn't study hard enough."

19. B
Here the word "sale" is used as a "word" and not as a word in the sentence, so quotation marks are used.

20. C
Titles of short stories are enclosed in quotation marks, and commas always go inside quotation marks.

21. A
Quoted speech is not capitalized.

22. B
The verb raise ('to increase', 'to lift up.') can appear in three forms, raise, raised and raised.

23. C
The two verbs "shall" and "will" should not be used in the same sentence when referring to the same future.

24. B
When two subjects are linked with "with" or "as well," use the verb form that matches the first subject.

25. A
Use a plural verb for nouns like measles, tongs, trousers, riches, scissors etc.

26. C
A verb can fit any of the two subjects in a compound sentence since the verb form agrees with that subject.

27. C
Always use the singular verb form for nouns like politics, wages, mathematics, innings, news, advice, summons, furniture, information, poetry, machinery, vacation, scenery etc.

28. C
Always use the singular verb form for nouns like politics, wages, mathematics, innings, news, advice, summons, furniture, information, poetry, machinery, vacation, scenery etc.

29. A
Use a singular verb with a plural noun that refers to a specific amount or quantity that is considered as a whole (dozen, hundred score etc).

30. C
Use a singular verb with either, each, neither, everyone and many.

ONLINE RESOURCES

How to Prepare for a Test - The Ultimate Guide

https://www.test-preparation.ca/the-ultimate-guide-to-test-preparation-strategy/

Learning Styles - The Complete Guide

https://www.test-preparation.ca/learning-styles/

Test Anxiety Secrets!

https://www.test-preparation.ca/how-to-overcome-test-anxiety/

Time Management on a Test

https://www.test-preparation.ca/test-tactics-the-time-wise-approach/

Flash Cards - The Complete Guide

https://www.test-preparation.ca/test-preparation-with-flash-cards/

Test Preparation Video Series

https://www.test-preparation.ca/video-series-on-test-preparation-multiple-choice-strategies-and-how-to-study/

How to Memorize - The Complete Guide

https://www.test-preparation.ca/a-guide-to-memorizing-anything-easily-and-painlessly/

Conclusion

Congratulations! You have made it this far because you have applied yourself diligently to practicing for the exam and no doubt improved your potential score considerably! Getting into a good school is a huge step in a journey that might be challenging at times but will be many times more rewarding and fulfilling. That is why being prepared is so important.

Good Luck!

Register for Free Updates and More Practice Test Questions

Register your purchase at https://www.test-preparation.ca/register/ for fast and convenient access to updates, errata, free test tips and more practice test questions.

https://www.facebook.com/CompleteTestPreparation/

https://www.youtube.com/user/MrTestPreparation

ONLINE RESOURCES

How to Prepare for a Test - The Ultimate Guide

https://www.test-preparation.ca/the-ultimate-guide-to-test-preparation-strategy/

Learning Styles - The Complete Guide

https://www.test-preparation.ca/learning-styles/

Test Anxiety Secrets!

https://www.test-preparation.ca/how-to-overcome-test-anxiety/

Time Management on a Test

https://www.test-preparation.ca/test-tactics-the-time-wise-approach/

Flash Cards - The Complete Guide

https://www.test-preparation.ca/test-preparation-with-flash-cards/

Test Preparation Video Series

https://www.test-preparation.ca/video-series-on-test-preparation-multiple-choice-strategies-and-how-to-study/

How to Memorize - The Complete Guide

https://www.test-preparation.ca/a-guide-to-memorizing-anything-easily-and-painlessly/

www.ingramcontent.com/pod-product-compliance
Lightning Source LLC
LaVergne TN
LVHW010255260326
834688LV00044B/1288